...ian

Cookbook

TARRAGON

The Vegetarian Pasta Cookbook

A superb selection of delicious and nutritious pasta dishes

SARAH MAXWELL

CHARTWELL
BOOKS, INC.

A QUINTET BOOK

Published by Chartwell Books
A Division of Book Sales, Inc.
114 Northfield Avenue
Edison, New Jersey 08837

This edition produced for sale in the U.S.A., its
territories and dependencies only.

First paperback edition published 1996.

Reprinted 1997

ISBN 0-7858-0650-4

This book was designed and produced by
Quintet Publishing Limited
6 Blundell Street
London N7 9BH

Creative Director: Richard Dewing
Designer: Ian Hunt
Project Editor: Katie Preston
Editor: Diana Vowles
Illustrator: Shona Cameron
Photographer: Tim Hill
Home Economist: Sarah Maxwell
Assistant Home Economist: Teresa Goldfinch

Typeset in Great Britain by
Central Southern Typesetters, Eastbourne
Manufactured in Singapore by
Eray Scan Pte. Ltd.
Printed in Hong Kong by
Sing Cheong Printing Co. Ltd.

DEDICATION
For Paul and Oliver
And with special thanks for my mum, Jenny

Contents

Introduction

TORTELLINI

The Vegetarian Pasta Cookbook provides you with exciting, new, and interesting recipes, some of which are quick and simple to prepare, while others require a little extra time and effort for those special-occasion meals. Whether you're cooking for a group of vegetarian guests or the odd one out in the family, these recipes will give you plenty of mouth-watering ideas.

The chapters have been divided into categories of ingredients for quick and easy reference – so when you have a yen for pasta with tomatoes, for example, simply turn to Pasta with Tomatoes and there are plenty of variations to choose from. There are recipes for all occasions, from fast family suppers to

BELOW *Three flavors of fresh pasta noodles ready for storing.*

formal food for friends. So take the plunge and boil up some pasta to be turned into a delicious vegetarian feast.

A word about the final chapter, Pasta Desserts. Don't be shy – have a go, and you (and your guests) are guaranteed to be pleasantly surprised.

The vegetarian issue

Although this book is predominantly suited to the lacto-vegetarian, there are a few vegan recipes also included.

Vegetarian cheeses made with vegetable rennet are becoming increasingly available in many different flavors and textures. If the particular cheeses recommended in the recipes are not available in a vegetarian form, you can simply use another type.

A point to note is to beware of certain colored pastas that are not vegetarian. For example, black pasta will probably be dyed with squid ink.

P A S T A

Pasta is one of man's earliest culinary inventions, dating back to over 3,000 years ago when the ancient Greeks recorded it in manuscripts and paintings, showing it to be one of the staple foods in their diet. Greece and Italy are not the only countries with a history of pasta making – the tradition also exists in Spain, Israel, and even Russia.

Pasta (which means paste in Italian) is generally made from semolina, durum or hard wheat mixed with water and/or oil and sometimes eggs. The dough is kneaded and rolled or extruded commercially to produce a myriad of shapes and sizes.

Fresh pasta is becoming even more available in many different varieties, not only from delicatessens (where the pasta is often made on the premises) but also from major supermarkets, where it can be found in packets in the chilled cabinets.

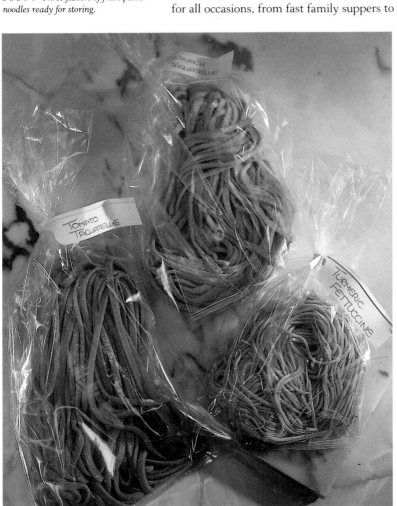

ABOVE *A pasta machine with an attachment for making stuffed pasta.*

The type of complex carbohydrates found in pasta makes it a good energy food, providing the body with a steady flow of energy as the carbohydrates are broken down during the process of digestion.

Mix and match

It is a case of personal preference when it comes to choosing a particular pasta shape to match your favorite pasta sauce. You may prefer small gnocchi (shells) to scoop up a rich tomato sauce, and tagliatelle or linguini for serving with a thick, creamy sauce, where each strand of pasta can be evenly coated in the sauce for a perfect combination of flavor and texture.

There continues to be great confusion over certain names for certain shapes of pasta. Suffice it to say that if you are able to describe its shape rather than remember its name, you are more likely to get what you are after!

Nutrition

Contrary to popular belief, pasta is not a fattening food. It is actually said to be quite low in calories and high in fiber, B vitamins and minerals such as potassium and iron.

ROTELLE

RIGHT *Freshly prepared farfalle (pasta bows).*

Pasta Dough ✓

This is the basic recipe referred to throughout the book. The dough can be made up to 2 days in advance, if kept airtight in the fridge. Bring the dough to room temperature before rolling out.

Freezing pasta is best done after it has been rolled out and cut into the required shape. Cook from frozen, allowing a little extra cooking time for stuffed pasta shapes.

MAKES ABOUT 1¼ LB

3 cups all-purpose flour
1 tbsp salt
4 tbsp sunflower oil
1 tbsp water
3 eggs

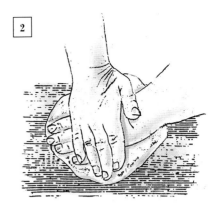

2

Turn out onto a lightly floured surface and knead the dough for about 5 minutes, adding the minimum amount of extra flour to stop the dough sticking, if necessary.

Place the dough in a plastic bag or seal in plastic wrap and leave to rest, at room temperature, for at least 30 minutes.

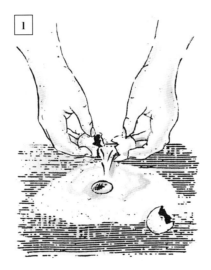

1

In a large mixing bowl, combine the flour and salt. Make a well in the center. In a small bowl, combine the sunflower oil and water and beat well. Break the eggs into the well, and add the oil and water mixture gradually. Mix until the dough forms clumps.

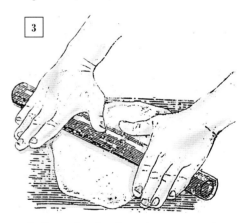

3

Roll out the dough, and cut to any shape you require.

TIPS FOR COOKING PERFECT PASTA:

- Use good-quality pasta.

- Use a saucepan that is large enough to hold the pasta with the water and still have at least one third of the saucepan free.

- Bring the water to the boil before adding the pasta, then simmer for the duration of the cooking time.

- Add a dash of oil to the cooking water to help prevent the pasta sticking together.

- Cook the pasta until *al dente,* or until just tender.

- To halt the cooking process, drain the pasta through a sieve and rinse under cold running water.

BASIC SAUCES

These basic sauces are used in recipes throughout the book. However, they can also be used as recipes in their own right, poured over or mixed into your favorite pasta shapes. Made up to two days in advance and kept, covered in the refrigerator, the sauces can be reheated for use in the recipes.

Cheese Sauce ✓

This sauce will keep in the fridge for up to a week.

Use for lasagnes, bakes, toppings, and fillings.

MAKES ABOUT 2½ CUPS

2 tbsp butter or margarine

¼ cup all-purpose flour

2½ cups warm milk

1 tsp Dijon mustard

1½ cups grated mature Cheddar cheese

salt and freshly ground black pepper

Melt the butter or margarine in a medium-sized saucepan, and stir in the flour. Cook for 30 seconds, then remove from the heat.

Stir in the milk, a little at a time, blending well after each addition to prevent any lumps. Return the sauce to a medium heat, and stir constantly until the sauce thickens and boils.

Add the mustard and cheese, and season to taste with salt and freshly ground black pepper. Continue to cook, stirring constantly, until the cheese has melted.

VARIATIONS:

MUSHROOM SAUCE Omit the mustard and cheese, and stir in 6oz/ 1½ cups chopped button mushrooms that have been sautéed in a little olive oil with a clove of crushed garlic and a pinch of dried thyme.

TOMATO SAUCE Omit the mustard and cheese, and stir in 3 tbsp tomato paste.

RAVIOLI

Pesto Sauce

This traditional Italian sauce should be used in moderation as it has a very strong flavor. Delicious stirred into fresh pasta, Pesto Sauce can also be used as an ingredient, added to other sauces and dishes. The texture of the finished pesto can be left relatively coarse or puréed until smooth.

SERVES 4–6

2 cloves of garlic, crushed

8 tbsp chopped, fresh basil

2 tbsp chopped, fresh parsley

scant ½ cup pine nuts

1 cup fresh, grated Parmesan cheese

⅔ cup extra virgin olive oil

salt and freshly ground black pepper

Place all the ingredients in a food processor or blender, and blend until the pesto reaches the desired texture.

Stir Pesto Sauce into freshly cooked pasta tossed in butter and freshly ground black pepper. Serve immediately with extra freshly grated Parmesan cheese.

TIP:
For a more traditional method of preparation, place all the ingredients in a mortar and use the pestle to grind and pound until the pesto reaches the desired texture.

BASIL

Cream Sauce

An excellent standby sauce for any occasion. It is delicious served with spaghetti, or used as a foundation for other ingredients to make a more elaborate dish.

SERVES 4

2 cloves of garlic, crushed

3 tbsp chopped, fresh parsley

1¼ cups light cream

salt and freshly ground black pepper

Place all the ingredients in a medium-sized frying pan and cook over low heat for 5–8 minutes, stirring occasionally.

SERVING SUGGESTION:
Stir Cream Sauce into freshly cooked tagliatelle verde, and serve immediately with plenty of freshly grated Parmesan cheese.

PARSLEY

1 **Pasta** *with Mushrooms*

Nutty Mushroom Bake

Most types of pasta work well for the topping of this dish; try spaghetti or tagliatelle instead of pennoni.

SERVES 4

2 cups dried pennoni (quills)

dash of olive oil, plus 2 tbsp

2 tbsp butter

1 onion, chopped

1 clove of garlic, crushed

2 tsp dried oregano

generous ½lb cup mushrooms, sliced

14oz can chopped tomatoes

1 heaped tbsp tomato paste

⅓ cup pimento-stuffed green olives, sliced

¾ cup roasted cashews

salt and freshly ground black pepper

1½ cups grated mature Cheddar cheese

Bring a large saucepan of water to the boil, and add the pennoni with a dash of olive oil. Cook for about 10 minutes, stirring occasionally, until tender. Drain, return to the saucepan, and stir in the butter until melted. Set aside, covered.

Preheat the oven to 400°F. Heat the remaining oil in a large frying pan and sauté the onion, garlic, and oregano for 3 minutes, or until the onion has softened.

Add the sliced mushrooms, and cook for a further 5 minutes, stirring occasionally. Stir in the chopped tomatoes and the tomato paste. Cover, and cook for about 10 minutes, stirring occasionally.

Add the sliced olives and the cashews, and season with salt and freshly ground black pepper. Continue to cook for a final 2–3 minutes, then transfer the mixture to a shallow, ovenproof dish. Spoon the buttered pasta on top, and sprinkle with the cheese. Bake for 20 minutes, or until crisp and golden.

Herby Mushroom Pasta Salad

Any small pasta shapes would be suitable for this dish. It can be served as a filling main course at lunchtime, or as an accompaniment.

SERVES 4–8

1lb dried pasta shapes

dash of olive oil

½lb cup mushrooms, quartered

1 red pepper, deseeded and cut into ½-inch squares

1 yellow pepper, deseeded and cut into ½-inch squares

1 cup pitted black olives

4 tbsp chopped, fresh basil

2 tbsp chopped, fresh parsley

FOR THE DRESSING:

2 tsp red wine vinegar

1 tsp salt

freshly ground black pepper

4 tbsp extra virgin olive oil

1 clove of garlic, crushed

1–2 tsp Dijon mustard

Bring a large saucepan of water to the boil, and add the pasta shapes with a dash of olive oil. Cook for about 10 minutes, stirring occasionally, until tender. Drain, and rinse under cold running water. Drain well again.

Place the cooked pasta shapes in a large salad bowl, and add the remaining salad ingredients. Mix well to combine.

To make the dressing, place all the ingredients in a screw-top jar and shake well. Pour the dressing over the salad and toss together.

Cover and refrigerate for at least 30 minutes, then toss again before serving.

Clear Cep Soup

This is a formal soup for special occasions. It has a strong mushroom flavor with the delicate addition of vegetables and pasta to create the contrasting textures.

SERVES 4

1oz dried ceps

2½ cups warm water

1 leek

1 carrot

1 cup conchigliette piccole (tiny pasta shells), cooked

salt and freshly ground black pepper

flat parsley leaves to garnish

Place the ceps in the warm water, and leave to soak for about 30 minutes. Drain the ceps, reserving the liquid in a saucepan.

Slice the ceps, and shred the leek and carrot. Add the vegetables to the mushroom stock and cook over medium heat for about 10 minutes, until the vegetables are tender. Add the cooked pasta shells, and season with salt and freshly ground black pepper. Cook for a further minute. Serve garnished with parsley leaves.

Farfalle with Fontina

Fontina cheese is available from most good cheese shops and gives this dish a creamy, subtle flavor. Although Emmental cheese is not a perfect substitute, it is more readily available and can be used as a good alternative.

SERVES 4

¾lb/4 cups dried farfalle (bows)

dash of olive oil

⅓ cup butter

1 onion, finely chopped

3 tbsp chopped, fresh basil

½lb cup mushrooms, sliced

14oz can chopped tomatoes

½lb coarsely grated Fontina cheese

salt and freshly ground black pepper

Bring a large saucepan of water to the boil, and add the farfalle with a dash of olive oil. Cook for about 10 minutes, stirring occasionally, until tender. Drain and set aside, covered, to keep warm.

Melt the butter in a large frying pan and sauté the onion and basil for about 5 minutes, until the onion is tender but not browned.

Stir the mushrooms into the onion mixture and continue to cook for a further 5–8 minutes, stirring frequently, until the mushrooms begin to brown.

Add the chopped tomatoes to the mushroom mixture, and cook for 1–2 minutes. Stir in the cheese, and season to taste with salt and freshly ground black pepper. Cook for a further 3–4 minutes, until the cheese has melted. Serve with the cooked farfalle.

FARFALLE

Clear Cep Soup

Pasta-topped Mushrooms

This dish is delicious served cold with a crisp, leafy salad, or warm as an appetizer or an accompaniment. The topping can be made in advance and arranged on the mushrooms at the last minute.

SERVES 2–4

¼ cup dried small stellette (stars)

dash of olive oil

4 large flat mushrooms

¼ cup butter

1 clove of garlic, crushed

½ yellow pepper, deseeded and finely diced

½ orange pepper, deseeded and finely diced

generous ¼lb blue cheese, such as Stilton or Danish blue, crumbled

salt and freshly ground black pepper

2 tbsp chopped, fresh parsley

Bring a large saucepan of water to the boil, and add the stellette with a dash of olive oil. Cook for about 7 minutes, stirring occasionally, until tender. Drain and set aside.

Cut the stalks out of the mushrooms and discard. Arrange the mushrooms, stalk side up, on a baking sheet and set aside.

To make the topping, melt the butter in a frying pan, and sauté the garlic for about 2 minutes. Add the diced peppers, and cook for a further 5–7 minutes. Stir in the crumbled blue cheese, and season to taste with salt and freshly ground black pepper. Add the parsley and stellette. Stir well.

Top each mushroom with the pasta mixture, then place the baking sheet in the broiler for 2–5 minutes, or until the topping is lightly golden and the mushrooms are warmed through.

Tagliatelle with Mushrooms

A quick supper for any occasion. Try using spaghetti or linguini for a change.

SERVES 4

1lb dried tagliatelle

dash of olive oil

2 tbsp butter

1 clove of garlic, crushed

2 tbsp chopped, fresh parsley

½lb button or cup mushrooms, sliced

salt and freshly ground black pepper

1¼ cups light cream

freshly grated Parmesan cheese, to serve

Bring a large saucepan of water to the boil, and add the tagliatelle with a dash of olive oil. Cook for about 10 minutes, stirring occasionally, until tender. Drain and set aside.

Meanwhile, melt the butter in a large frying pan, and sauté the garlic and chopped parsley for 2–3 minutes. Add the sliced mushrooms and cook for 5–8 minutes, or until softened and slightly browned.

Season the mushroom mixture with salt and freshly ground black pepper, then stir in the cream. Cook the sauce for 1–2 minutes, then stir in the tagliatelle. Continue to cook while stirring to coat the tagliatelle in the sauce. Serve with plenty of freshly grated Parmesan cheese.

OPPOSITE *Pasta-topped Mushrooms*

CEP

Fusilli with Wild Mushrooms

Wild mushrooms, or ceps, are increasingly available and are the special ingredient in this dish. Dried ceps can be found in Italian delicatessens; they need to be soaked in water for 30 minutes before using in the recipe.

SERVES 4

¾lb/3½ cups dried long fusilli (twists)

dash of olive oil plus ¼ cup

1 clove of garlic, crushed

2 tbsp chopped, fresh thyme

generous ¼lb shiitake mushrooms, sliced

generous ¼lb oyster mushrooms

½oz dried ceps, soaked, drained, and sliced

salt and freshly ground black pepper

freshly grated Parmesan cheese, to serve

Bring a large saucepan of water to the boil, and add the fusilli with a dash of olive oil. Cook for about 10 minutes, stirring occasionally, until tender. Drain and set aside, covered.

Heat the olive oil in a large frying pan, and add the garlic and fresh thyme. Cook for 1–2 minutes, then stir in all the mushrooms and season to taste with salt and freshly ground black pepper.

Fry the mushroom mixture over high heat for 3–4 minutes to brown slightly, then turn the mixture into the saucepan containing the fusilli. Toss together briefly, then serve with a little freshly grated Parmesan cheese.

FIELD

Cheesy Mushroom Canapés

These tasty morsels are ideal for entertaining. They can be made in advance, and are delicious served with drinks.

CONCHIGLIE

SERVES 8–10

20 dried large lumache rigate or large shells

dash of olive oil

3 tbsp freshly grated Parmesan cheese

FOR THE FILLING:

2 tbsp olive oil

1 clove of garlic, chopped

1 small onion, finely chopped

3 tbsp chopped, fresh parsley

6oz/1½ cups button mushrooms, very finely chopped

⅓ cup pitted olives, very finely chopped

½lb cream cheese

salt and freshly ground black pepper

Bring a large saucepan of water to the boil, and add the pasta with a dash of olive oil. Cook for about 10 minutes, stirring occasionally, until tender. Drain, and rinse under cold running water. Pat dry with paper towels, and set aside.

To make the filling, heat the oil in a large frying pan, and sauté the garlic and onion for about 3 minutes, until softened. Remove from the heat, and stir in the remaining filling ingredients.

Use a teaspoon to stuff each pasta shape with the filling, then arrange them on a baking sheet. Sprinkle with grated Parmesan cheese, and place in the broiler for about 5 minutes until golden. Arrange on a serving platter.

Creamy Mushroom Pasta Pie

A dish that is perfect for a romantic dinner for two. It can be made in advance and simply reheated to serve, so that you won't be tied to the kitchen.

SERVES 2

1lb puff pastry, thawed if frozen

milk, to glaze

FOR THE FILLING:

2 cups dried, wholewheat pasta shells

dash of olive oil

2 tbsp butter

1 clove of garlic, crushed

5oz/1¼ cups button mushrooms, sliced

about 12 baby corn, cut into chunks

⅓ cup all-purpose flour

⅔ cup milk

salt and freshly ground black pepper

¾ cup mature Cheddar cheese

chopped, fresh parsley, to garnish

Preheat the oven to 400°F. Roll the pastry out into two rectangular pieces, each measuring 6 × 4 inches. Set one rectangle aside to make the base of the pastry case. Take the other piece and cut out an inner rectangle using a ruler and a sharp knife, leaving a 1-inch border to make the rim of the pastry case. Reserve the inner rectangle to make the lid and, using a sharp knife, score it to make a pattern. Brush a little milk around the edges of the base of the pastry case, and place the rim in position on top.

Place on a baking sheet with the lid alongside, and brush all the surfaces with a little milk to glaze. Bake for about 15–20 minutes, or until well-risen and golden-brown. Remove from the oven, and transfer the pastry case to a wire rack to cool. If the center of the pastry case has risen too high, gently press down to create a hollow space. Place on a serving plate.

To make the filling, bring a large saucepan of water to the boil and add the wholewheat pasta shells with a dash of olive oil. Cook for about 10 minutes, stirring occasionally, until tender. Drain well and set aside.

Melt the butter in a large saucepan, and sauté the garlic, mushrooms, and baby corn for 5–8 minutes, or until softened. Stir in the flour, and mix to form a paste. Gradually stir in the milk, a little at a time, stirring well after each addition. Bring the sauce slowly to the boil, stirring constantly to prevent lumps from forming. Season with salt and freshly ground black pepper. Stir in the grated cheese and continue to cook for a further 2–3 minutes, until the cheese has melted.

Stir the pasta in the sauce, then spoon the sauce into the pastry case. Sprinkle with the chopped, fresh parsley, then place the lid on top and serve.

CONCHIGLIE

Mushroom Cannelloni

Cannelloni is a time-consuming dish to prepare, but it is always worth the effort. Cook more cannelloni pasta than is required to allow for any split ones.

SERVES 4

8 dried cannelloni tubes

dash of olive oil

butter, for greasing

1 quantity Mushroom Sauce (page 9)

FOR THE FILLING:

2 tbsp olive oil

1 clove of garlic, crushed

1 onion, finely chopped

1 tbsp chopped, fresh thyme

½lb button mushrooms, finely chopped

½ cup fine, fresh breadcrumbs

salt and freshly ground black pepper

Bring a large saucepan of water to the boil, and add the cannelloni with a dash of olive oil. Cook for about 10 minutes, stirring occasionally, until tender. Drain and rinse under cold running water. Pat dry with paper towels and set aside.

To make the filling, heat the oil in a large frying pan and sauté the garlic, onion, and thyme for about 3 minutes, or until the onion has softened.

Add the chopped mushrooms to the onion mixture and continue to cook for about 10 minutes, stirring frequently. Add the breadcrumbs, and season with salt and freshly ground black pepper. Stir well.

Preheat the oven to 400°F. Butter the inside of an ovenproof casserole dish. Using a teaspoon, stuff each cannelloni with the filling, then lay it in the dish.

Pour the Mushroom Sauce evenly over the cannelloni, then bake for about 30 minutes, until heated through and golden on top.

Mushroom Stroganoff with Pasta

A rich dinner-party dish that is delicious served with a glass of chilled dry white wine.

SERVES 4–6

¼ cup butter

2 cloves of garlic, crushed

1 onion, sliced into thin wedges

1½lb mixed mushrooms (oyster, maron, cup, etc), left whole or cut in half

3 level tbsp all-purpose flour

⅔ cup vegetable broth

3 tbsp dry white wine

salt and freshly ground black pepper

⅓ cup heavy cream

3 tbsp chopped, fresh thyme

2 tbsp paprika

1½lb cooked tagliatelle, tossed in butter, to serve

Melt the butter in a large saucepan, and sauté the garlic and onion for about 7 minutes, until the onion has browned slightly.

Add the mushrooms and cook for 2 minutes, then stir in the flour. Cook for 30 seconds, then gradually stir in the vegetable broth, then the wine. Bring the sauce to the boil, and season with salt and freshly ground black pepper. Stir in the cream, fresh thyme, and paprika. Cook for a further 2 minutes, then serve with hot, buttered tagliatelle.

OYSTER

Deep-fried Mushroom Pasta Pockets

Serve this dish as an appetizer with a small dish of Garlic Mayonnaise (see Tip) for dipping.

SERVES 4–6

½lb fresh lasagne noodles

1 egg, beaten

sunflower oil, for deep-frying

FOR THE FILLING:

½lb cream cheese with herbs and garlic

6oz/1½ cups button mushrooms

Lay the fresh lasagne noodles out on the work surface, and stamp out rounds using a 3-inch cutter.

Place the cream cheese and the mushrooms in a food processor, and blend to form a coarse texture.

Spoon some of the mushroom mixture onto one half of each pasta round. Brush a little of the beaten egg around the edges of the rounds, then fold in half to encase the filling, sealing firmly with your fingers. Lay the mushroom pockets out on baking sheets, and chill in the refrigerator for 30 minutes.

Heat the oil for deep frying, and fry the mushroom pockets in batches for about 3 minutes, until crisp and golden. Remove from the oil and drain on paper towels. Place on a baking sheet, and keep warm in a low oven until all the batches are cooked. Serve with Garlic Mayonnaise for dipping.

TIP:
To make Garlic Mayonnaise, mix 4 cloves of garlic, crushed, with 1¼ cups mayonnaise. Chill for 30 minutes before serving.

Mushroom Stroganoff with Pasta.

Pinwheel Pasta Bake.

Pinwheel Pasta Bake ✓

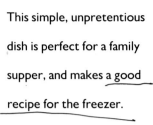

This simple, unpretentious dish is perfect for a family supper, and makes a good recipe for the freezer. When thawed, reheat, covered, in a medium-hot oven.

SERVES 4–6

1½lb dried rotelle (pinwheels)

dash of olive oil

2 tbsp sunflower oil

1 clove of garlic, crushed

½lb mushrooms, quartered

¼lb zucchini, chopped

3 tbsp chopped, fresh parsley

⅔ cup vegetable broth

2¼ cups grated mature Cheddar cheese

Bring a large saucepan of water to the boil, and add the rotelle with a dash of olive oil. Cook for about 10 minutes, sitrring occasionally, until tender. Drain, and set aside.

Heat the sunflower oil in a large frying pan, and sauté the garlic for 2 minutes. Add the mushrooms and zucchini, and cook, covered, for 5 minutes, or until softened.

Stir the chopped parsley and vegetable broth into the mushroom mixture, and continue to cook, covered, for a further 10 minutes. Add the rotelle, and stir in the grated cheese.

Preheat the oven to 400°F. Transfer the pasta mixture to a deep casserole dish, and bake for about 20 minutes. Serve with warm, crusty bread.

ROTELLE

Hearty Cream of Mushroom Soup ✓

Perfect for a cold winter's night or even a filling lunchtime dish. Serve with warm, crusty garlic bread for a more substantial meal.

SERVES 4

2 tbsp butter

1 onion, finely chopped

¾lb cup mushrooms, finely chopped

1 tbsp all-purpose flour

2½ cups vegetable broth

1¼ cups milk

salt and freshly ground black pepper

½ cup cooked tiny pasta shapes

pinch of freshly grated nutmeg

Melt the butter in a large saucepan, and sauté the onion for about 3 minutes until softened. Add the chopped mushrooms, cover, and cook for a further 5 minutes.

Stir in the flour, then gradually add the broth and milk, stirring well after each addition. Cover, and cook for 15–20 minutes, stirring occasionally. Season with salt and freshly ground black pepper. Stir in the pasta shapes and grated nutmeg. Cook for a final 2–3 minutes, then serve.

Mushroom Ravioli

Once you have tasted fresh, homemade ravioli, not only will you never buy it ready-made again, but you will probably want to invest in a ravioli pan, which will make future ravioli-making even easier.

⅔ quantity Pasta Dough (page 8)

1 quantity Mushroom Sauce (page 9)

SERVES 6

⅔ quantity Pasta Dough (page 8)

1 quantity Mushroom Sauce (page 9)

1 egg, beaten, for brushing

dash of olive oil

chopped, fresh parsley, to garnish

freshly grated Parmesan cheese, to serve

FOR THE FILLING:

2 tbsp olive oil

1 clove of garlic, crushed

3 tbsp chopped, fresh thyme

½lb button mushrooms, finely chopped

1 cup fine, fresh white breadcrumbs

salt and freshly ground black pepper

Keep the fresh pasta dough covered in plastic wrap at room temperature and the Mushroom Sauce in a saucepan, ready to reheat later.

To make the filling, heat the oil in a large frying pan and add the garlic and fresh thyme. Cook for 1–2 minutes, then stir in the mushrooms and fry for 3–5 minutes. Stir in the breadcrumbs, and season to taste with salt and freshly ground black pepper.

Remove from the heat and allow to cool completely.

To make the ravioli, cut the pasta dough in half. Roll out one half to a rectangle slightly larger than 14 × 10 inches. Trim the edges of the dough neatly. Cover the rectangle with plastic wrap to prevent it drying out. Roll out the other half of the dough to the same measurements. Do not trim the edges.

Place half teaspoonfuls of the filling mixture in lines, spaced about ¾ inch apart, all over the trimmed rectangle of pasta dough. Brush the beaten egg lightly in lines around the filling mixture to make the square shapes for the ravioli.

Lay the other rectangle of pasta dough on top and, starting at one end, seal in the filling by lightly pressing the dough, pushing out any trapped air and gently flattening the filling, to make little packets. Using a sharp knife or a pastry wheel, cut down and across in lines around the filling to make the square ravioli.

To cook the ravioli, bring a large saucepan of water to the boil and add the ravioli with a dash of olive oil. Cook for about 6 minutes, stirring occasionally, until tender. Drain.

Meanwhile, reheat the Mushroom Sauce. Serve the Mushroom Ravioli with the Mushroom Sauce, sprinkled with chopped parsley and grated Parmesan cheese.

FIELD

2 **Pasta** *with Tomatoes*

Bucatini with Tomatoes

This is a vegetarian version of a simple yet classic Italian dish. Use Parmesan cheese if Pecorino is not available.

SERVES 4

¾lb dried bucatini (long tubes)

dash of olive oil

2 cloves of garlic, crushed

1 onion, finely chopped

1lb carton sieved tomatoes

4 tbsp chopped, fresh basil

salt and freshly ground black pepper

butter, for greasing

⅔ cup freshly grated Pecorino or Parmesan cheese

Bring a large saucepan of water to the boil, and add the bucatini with a dash of olive oil. Cook for about 10 minutes, stirring occasionally, until tender. Drain and set aside.

Preheat the oven to 400°F. Place the garlic, onion, sieved tomatoes, basil, and salt and freshly ground black pepper in a large frying pan, and heat until simmering. Cook for about 5 minutes, then remove from the heat.

Arrange the bucatini in a shallow, buttered, ovenproof dish. Curl it around to fit the dish, adding one or two tubes at a time, until the dish is tightly packed with the pasta.

Spoon the tomato mixture over the top, prodding the pasta to ensure the sauce sinks down to the bottom of the dish. Sprinkle with the grated cheese, and bake for 25–30 minutes, until bubbling, crisp, and golden. Cut in wedges, like a cake, to serve.

YELLOW CHERRY

Tagliatelle Neapolitan

Yellow tomatoes make this dish look particularly attractive, though red ones taste just as good. If you can't find fresh tagliatelle, use the dried egg version.

SERVES 4

1lb fresh, multicolored tagliatelle

dash of olive oil, plus 2 tbsp

2 cloves of garlic, crushed

1 onion, chopped

3 tbsp chopped, fresh basil or oregano

1lb yellow and red tomatoes, skinned, deseeded, and chopped

8oz carton sieved tomatoes

salt and freshly ground black pepper

fresh basil, to garnish

freshly grated Parmesan cheese, to serve

Bring a large saucepan of water to the boil, and add the tagliatelle with a dash of olive oil. Cook for about 5 minutes, stirring occasionally, until tender. Drain and set aside, covered.

Heat the remaining oil in a large frying pan, and sauté the garlic, onion, and basil or oregano for about 3 minutes, or until the onion has softened.

Add the chopped tomato flesh and sieved tomatoes, and season with salt and freshly ground black pepper. Stir and cook for about 10 minutes, until thickened and bubbling. Serve with the tagliatelle. Garnish with fresh basil and sprinkle with freshly grated Parmesan cheese.

Tomato Tortellini with Tomato Basil Sauce

Although fresh tortellini is increasingly available in supermarkets and delicatessens, nothing tastes quite as good as real homemade pasta. Once the production line is assembled, with the pasta shapes cut out and the filling on standby, the process is simple, efficient, and fun!

TORTELLINI

SERVES 6–8

⅔ quantity Pasta Dough (page 8) with 1 tbsp tomato paste beaten into the eggs

1 egg, beaten for brushing

dash of olive oil

chopped, fresh basil, to garnish

freshly grated Parmesan cheese, to serve

FOR THE FILLING:

14oz can chopped tomatoes, drained

2 cloves of garlic, crushed

1¾ cups fresh breadcrumbs

3 tbsp chopped, fresh basil

salt and freshly ground black pepper

FOR THE SAUCE:

2 tbsp olive oil

1 clove of garlic, crushed

1 small onion, very finely chopped

14oz can chopped tomatoes

2 tbsp tomato paste

4 tbsp chopped, fresh basil

salt and freshly ground black pepper

Wrap the pasta dough in plastic wrap to prevent it from drying out, and set aside.

To make the filling, mix all the ingredients together in a medium-sized bowl and set aside, covered.

To make the sauce, heat the olive oil in a large saucepan, and sauté the garlic and onion for about 5 minutes, until softened. Add the remaining sauce ingredients and simmer for 10–15 minutes, until bubbling and thickened. Set aside, covered, to keep warm.

To make the tortellini, cut the pasta dough in half. Keep one portion covered with plastic wrap, and roll out the other portion to a 12-inch square. Cut the dough into six 2-inch strips. Now cut the strips into 2-inch squares, and brush each one with a little beaten egg.

Place a little of the tomato filling on each pasta square, then fold the squares over into triangles. Seal the edges, then wrap the long side of the triangle around the tip of your forefinger and pinch the corners together tightly. Continue sealing and shaping the tortellini, then roll out the other half of the pasta dough and repeat the process. Place the filled tortellini on baking sheets lined with waxed paper.

To cook the tortellini, bring a large saucepan of water to the boil and add the pasta with a dash of olive oil. Cook for about 5 minutes, stirring occasionally, until tender. Drain and set aside, covered, to keep warm.

Reheat the sauce and serve with the tortellini, garnished with chopped, fresh basil and sprinkled with freshly grated Parmesan cheese.

> **TIP:**
> Do not overfill the tortellini with stuffing or they may split during cooking.

Fusilli with Sun-dried Tomatoes

A dish that is delicious served warm as a main course or cold as a summer salad. Tomato pesto is widely available.

SERVES 2–4

1lb dried fusilli (twists)

dash of olive oil, plus extra for drizzling

2 tbsp tomato pesto

6oz jar sun-dried tomatoes, drained and chopped

4 plum tomatoes, sliced into wedges

4 tbsp chopped, fresh basil

salt and freshly ground black pepper

Bring a large saucepan of water to the boil, and add the fusilli with a dash of olive oil. Cook for about 10 minutes, stirring occasionally, until tender. Drain and return to the saucepan.

Stir in the remaining ingredients, drizzle with olive oil and serve warm immediately, or cool and refrigerate to serve chilled, if preferred.

OPPOSITE *Fusilli with Sun-dried Tomatoes.*

Spicy Stuffed Tomatoes

Beefsteak tomatoes are perfect for stuffing. Serve as a vegetable accompaniment or as an appetizer. To make the tomatoes stand up in the dish, slice a thin shaving off the bottom of each one.

SERVES 4

½ cup dried pastina (any tiny shapes)

dash of olive oil

4 large beefsteak tomatoes

butter, for greasing

FOR THE FILLING:

2 medium potatoes, cut into ¼-inch cubes

4 tbsp olive oil

2 cloves of garlic, crushed

1 onion, finely chopped

2 tsp mild curry powder

pinch of ground cumin

1 tbsp tomato paste

4 tbsp chopped, fresh coriander

salt and freshly ground black pepper

Bring a saucepan of water to the boil, and add the pastina with a dash of olive oil. Cook for about 8 minutes, stirring occasionally, until tender. Drain and set aside.

Slice the tops off the tomatoes and reserve for the lids. Using a teaspoon, scrape out the flesh of each tomato and reserve. Arrange the hollowed tomatoes in a buttered, oven-proof dish and set aside.

To make the filling, cook the potatoes in boiling water for about 10 minutes, until tender. Drain and set aside. Heat the olive oil in a large frying pan, and sauté the garlic and onion for about 3 minutes, until softened.

Add the curry powder, cumin, and tomato paste. Cook for 2 minutes, then gently stir in the pastina and cooked potato. Add the chopped coriander, and season with salt and freshly ground black pepper. Cook for a further 2–3 minutes, stirring occasionally, then remove from the heat.

Preheat the oven to 400°F. Stuff the tomatoes with the filling, placing any extra in the bottom of the dish. Place the tomato lids on top and bake for about 20 minutes, or until heated through.

BEEFSTEAK

Italian Spaghettini

Italian Spaghettini ✓

Pine nuts give this dish its special taste and texture. Serve it straight from the pan.

PLUM

SERVES 4

1lb dried multicolored spaghettini

dash of olive oil

¼ cup butter

1 clove of garlic, crushed

1 small onion, very finely chopped

⅔ cup pine nuts

8oz carton sieved tomatoes

salt and freshly ground black pepper

4 tbsp chopped, fresh basil

2 tbsp chopped, fresh parsley

Bring a large saucepan of water to the boil, and add the dried spaghettini with a dash of olive oil. Cook for about 10 minutes, stirring occasionally, until tender. Drain, and set aside.

Melt the butter in a large frying pan and sauté the garlic and onion for about 3 minutes, or until the onion has softened. Add the pine nuts and stir-fry until evenly golden.

Add the sieved tomatoes, herbs, and salt and freshly ground black pepper, and cook for about 5 minutes, stirring occasionally.

Add the spaghettini, and stir well to coat in the tomato sauce. Cook for a further 5 minutes, then serve immediately.

Fettuccine with Tomatoes and Mozzarella

This delicious summertime salad can be made well in advance and left to marinate for up to 3 hours.

SERVES 4

¾lb dried egg fettuccine

dash of olive oil

1lb (about 2 medium) beefsteak tomatoes, skinned, deseeded, and sliced

5 tbsp extra virgin olive oil

2 cloves of garlic, crushed

6 tbsp chopped, fresh basil

2 tbsp chopped, fresh oregano

¾lb mozzarella cheese, cut into ½-inch cubes

⅔ cup freshly grated Pecorino or Parmesan cheese

salt and freshly ground black pepper

Bring a large saucepan of water to the boil, and add the fettuccine with a dash of olive oil. Cook for about 10 minutes, stirring occasionally, until tender. Drain and rinse under cold running water. Drain again, and set aside.

In a large bowl, combine the sliced tomato flesh with the remaining ingredients and toss together lightly. Add the cooked fettuccine, and mix lightly to coat in the oil. Serve this salad at room temperature with warm garlic bread.

Pasta al Pomodoro

Any pasta shapes would be suitable for this recipe, so use whatever you have in the cupboard. The sauce is quick and simple, making this dish a perfect supper for unexpected guests.

STELLETTI

SERVES 4–6

1lb dried pasta

dash of olive oil

2 tbsp butter

2 cloves of garlic, crushed

1 onion, chopped

1lb carton sieved tomatoes

salt and freshly ground black pepper

fresh flat parsley sprigs, to garnish

slivers of fresh Parmesan cheese, to serve

Bring a saucepan of water to the boil, and add the pasta with a dash of olive oil. Cook for about 10 minutes, stirring occasionally, until tender. Drain and set aside, covered, to keep warm.

Melt the butter in a large frying pan, and sauté the garlic and onion for about 3 minutes, until softened. Stir in the tomatoes and season with salt and freshly ground black pepper. Simmer the sauce for about 10 minutes then serve with the pasta, garnished with parsley sprigs and sprinkled with slivers of fresh Parmesan cheese.

> **TIP:**
> To make slivers of Parmesan cheese, use a vegetable peeler.

Tomato Vegetable Crumble

A delicious, wholesome main-course dish. Serve with lightly cooked green beans tossed in butter and black pepper.

PLUM

SERVES 4–6

1lb dried macaroni

dash of olive oil, plus 2 tbsp

2 cloves of garlic, crushed

1 onion, chopped

4 tbsp chopped, fresh parsley

14oz can chopped tomatoes

1 medium tomato, chopped

2 tbsp tomato paste

salt and freshly ground black pepper

FOR THE TOPPING:

2¼ cups rolled oats

1 cup ground hazelnuts

⅔ cup freshly grated Parmesan cheese

1 tbsp dried thyme

⅓ cup butter

Bring a large saucepan of water to the boil, and add the macaroni with a dash of olive oil. Cook for about 10 minutes, stirring occasionally, until tender. Drain and set aside.

Heat the remaining olive oil in a large frying pan and sauté the garlic and onion for about 3 minutes, until softened. Add the parsley, chopped tomatoes, tomato paste, and salt and freshly ground black pepper. Cook for about 5 minutes, then stir in the macaroni. Turn the macaroni mixture into a shallow, ovenproof dish and set aside. Preheat the oven to 350°F.

To make the topping, combine all the ingredients in a mixing bowl and rub in the butter until the mixture resembles bread-crumbs. Scatter the topping over the tomato macaroni, and press down gently. Bake for about 30 minutes, until golden and heated through.

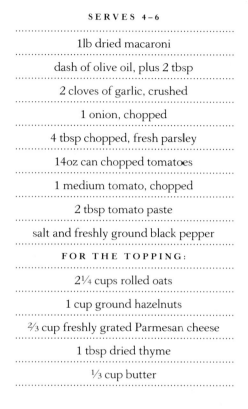

Macaroni Neapolitan ✓

A quick and delicious way to serve macaroni. Serve with a crisp green salad. You can make endless variations of this dish by using a different pasta shape each time you prepare it.

SERVES 4

1lb dried macaroni

dash of olive oil, plus ⅓ cup

2 cloves of garlic, crushed

4 tbsp chopped, fresh parsley

2 × 1lb cartons pulped tomatoes

1 tbsp tomato paste

salt and freshly ground black pepper

⅓ cup freshly grated Parmesan cheese

Bring a large saucepan of water to the boil, and add the macaroni with a dash of olive oil. Cook for about 10 minutes, stirring occasionally, until tender. Drain, and return to the saucepan to keep warm.

Preheat the oven to 400°F. Heat the remaining oil in a large frying pan and sauté the garlic with the parsley for 2–3 minutes, stirring frequently. Add the tomatoes, tomato paste and salt and freshly ground black pepper. Cook for about 10 minutes, stirring occasionally.

Stir the tomato sauce evenly into the macaroni, then transfer the mixture to an ovenproof dish. Sprinkle the Parmesan cheese over the top, and bake for about 30 minutes.

Tomato Pasta Timbales

An attractive first course, these timbales are very easy to make and are sure to impress your guests. Make them up to one hour in advance and place them in the oven to bake.

BEEFSTEAK

SERVES 4

¾lb dried, multicolored spaghettini

dash of olive oil, plus extra for greasing

4 small tomato slices

2 tbsp tomato pesto

2 eggs, beaten

¼ cup milk

salt and freshly ground black pepper

FOR THE SAUCE:

8oz carton sieved tomatoes

1 tbsp sweet soya sauce

4 tbsp chopped, fresh basil

salt and freshly ground black pepper

TO GARNISH:

fresh flat parsley sprigs

cherry tomatoes

Bring a large saucepan of water to the boil, and add the spaghettini with a dash of olive oil. Cook for about 10 minutes, stirring occasionally, until tender. Drain well.

Preheat the oven to 325°F. Grease four 6floz individual ovenproof molds with a little olive oil, and place a circle of waxed paper in the bottom of each. Place a slice of tomato in the base of each mold, then carefully pack in the spaghettini, leaving a ¼-inch space at the top.

In a small bowl, combine the tomato pesto, eggs, milk, and salt and freshly ground black pepper. Beat well then pour into each spaghettini mold, covering the pasta.

Arrange the molds in a roasting pan with enough boiling water to come halfway up the sides. Bake for about 40 minutes, until set and firm to the touch.

Meanwhile, to make the sauce, place all the ingredients in a saucepan and heat to simmering point. Simmer for 10 minutes, until thickened slightly.

Run a sharp knife around the edges of each timbale, then invert each onto individual plates. Pour a little sauce around each timbale, and garnish.

Tomato and Pasta Salad

Orecchiette are small, ear-shaped pasta. If they are not available, gnocchi pasta shapes (dumplings) will work just as well.

CONCHIGLIE

SERVES 6–8

1¼lb fresh orecchiette (ears)

dash of olive oil

1lb red and yellow tomatoes, chopped

6-inch piece cucumber, chopped

6oz feta cheese, chopped

5 tbsp chopped, fresh coriander

2 tbsp chopped, fresh basil

FOR THE DRESSING:

1 tbsp white wine vinegar

4 tbsp olive oil

2 cloves of garlic, crushed

salt and freshly ground black pepper

TO GARNISH:

cherry tomatoes

fresh coriander sprigs

Bring a large saucepan of water to the boil, and add the orecchiette with a dash of olive oil. Cook for about 5 minutes, stirring occasionally, until tender. Drain and rinse under cold running water. Drain again, and set aside.

Place the orecchiette in a large mixing bowl, and add the remaining salad ingredients. Mix to combine. To make the dressing, place all the ingredients in a screw-top jar and shake well. Pour the dressing over the salad, and toss to coat. Serve garnished with cherry tomatoes and coriander sprigs.

Tomato Mozzarella Kebabs

These are excellent for a vegetarian barbecue. Serve the kebabs with plenty of hot, crusty garlic bread and salad.

SERVES 4

1¼ cups dried rotelle (pinwheels)

dash of olive oil, plus 4 tbsp

2 cloves of garlic, crushed

salt and freshly ground black pepper

8–12 cherry tomatoes

½lb mozzarella cheese, cut into 1-inch cubes

YELLOW CHERRY

Bring a large saucepan of water to the boil, and add the rotelle with a dash of olive oil. Cook for about 10 minutes, stirring occasionally, until tender. Drain and rinse under cold running water. Drain again and set aside.

In a small bowl, combine the olive oil, garlic, and salt and freshly ground black pepper. Set aside.

To make the kebabs, place one rotelle, a tomato, then a cube of mozzarella cheese onto kebab skewers until all the ingredients have been used. Arrange the skewers on a baking sheet and brush liberally with the garlic olive oil mixture, turning the kebabs to coat evenly.

Place the kebabs in a preheated broiler for 5–7 minutes, turning the skewers halfway through cooking, until browned. Serve immediately.

> **TIP:**
> If using wooden skewers, soak them in water for at least one hour before threading on the kebab ingredients. This will help prevent them from burning during grilling.

Spaghettini with Tomato Ragout

This version of ragout is a brilliant standby sauce to use when hunger won't wait for time.

SERVES 4

1lb dried spaghettini

dash of olive oil

freshly grated Parmesan cheese, to serve

FOR THE RAGOUT:

2 tbsp butter

1 clove of garlic, crushed

1 large onion, finely chopped

14oz can chopped tomatoes

⅔ cup dry red wine

4 tbsp chopped, fresh basil

salt and freshly ground black pepper

Bring a large saucepan of water to the boil, and add the spaghettini with a dash of olive oil. Cook for about 10 minutes, stirring occasionally, until tender. Drain and set aside, covered, to keep warm.

To make the ragout, melt the butter in a large frying pan and sauté the garlic and onion for about 3 minutes, until softened. Add the remaining ragout ingredients, stir, and simmer for 15 minutes, until slightly thickened. Serve with the spaghettini, sprinkled with freshly grated Parmesan cheese.

OPPOSITE *Tomato Mozzarella Kebabs.*

Trenette with Tomato Tarragon Cream

This rich pasta dish which is not for the health conscious! However, it is extremely delicious with a glass of chilled dry white wine.

SERVES 4

1lb dried trenette (long, wavy strips)

dash of olive oil, plus 1 tbsp

2 cloves of garlic, crushed

4 tbsp chopped, fresh tarragon

½lb cherry tomatoes, halved

1¼ cups light cream

salt and freshly ground black pepper

freshly grated Parmesan cheese, to serve

Bring a large saucepan of water to the boil, and add the trenette with a dash of olive oil. Cook for about 10 minutes, stirring occasionally, until tender. Drain, and return to the saucepan. Set aside, covered, to keep warm.

Heat the remaining olive oil in a large frying pan, and add the garlic, tarragon, and tomatoes. Sauté for about 3 minutes, stirring occasionally, then stir in the cream. Season with salt and freshly ground black pepper and cook for 2–3 minutes, until heated through. Stir into the pasta, then serve with freshly grated Parmesan cheese.

3 **Pasta** *with Peppers*

Stuffed Peppers

A refreshing alternative to rice, pasta makes a perfect filling for peppers. Tiny pasta shapes also work well in this dish. Serve with a crisp green salad.

SERVES 4

½lb gnocchetti sardi (small dumpling shapes)

dash of olive oil

4 peppers, for stuffing

flat leaf parsley sprigs, to garnish

FOR THE FILLING:

¼ cup butter

6 scallions, finely chopped

2 cloves of garlic, crushed

1 pepper, deseeded and finely diced

salt and freshly ground black pepper

⅔ cup freshly grated Parmesan cheese

Bring a large saucepan of water to the boil, and add the gnocchetti sardi with a dash of olive oil. Cook for about 10 minutes, stirring occasionally, until tender. Drain and set aside.

Preheat the oven to 400°F. Lay each pepper on its side and slice off the top, reserving it to make the lid. Scoop out and discard the seeds and pith. Arrange the hollowed-out peppers in a shallow, ovenproof dish, and set aside.

To make the filling, melt the butter in a large frying pan and sauté the scallions and garlic for about 2 minutes, then add the diced pepper. Season with salt and freshly ground black pepper and cook for about 5 minutes, stirring occasionally.

Add the gnocchetti and the Parmesan cheese to the filling mixture, and cook for about 2 minutes to heat through. Using a dessertspoon, stuff each pepper with the pasta filling, scattering any extra around the edges.

Place the pepper lids in the dish and bake for about 30 minutes, until the peppers have softened. Just before serving, place in the broiler for 2–3 minutes to char the pepper skins, if desired. Serve garnished with parsley sprigs.

RED

Pepper and Pasta Ratatouille.

Pepper and Pasta Ratatouille

Served with a hot, buttered baked potato, this simple dish is perfectly delicious.

CONCHIGLIE

SERVES 4-6

1lb dried wholewheat gnocchi piccoli (small shells)

dash of olive oil, plus 3 tbsp

2 cloves of garlic, crushed

1 onion, chopped

2 green peppers, deseeded and cut into chunks

14oz can chopped tomatoes

2 heaped tbsp tomato paste

⅔ cup dry red wine

2 tbsp fresh oregano

salt and freshly ground black pepper

fresh oregano sprigs, to garnish

Bring a large saucepan of water to the boil, and add the gnocchi piccoli with a dash of olive oil. Cook for about 10 minutes, stirring occasionally, until tender. Drain and set aside.

Heat the remaining olive oil in a large saucepan and sauté the garlic and onion for about 3 minutes, until softened. Stir in the pepper chunks. Cover and cook for about 5 minutes, or until the pepper has softened slightly.

Stir in the remaining ingredients, except the oregano sprigs, into the pepper mixture and bring to simmering point. Reduce the heat, cover, and cook for about 10 minutes, then stir in the gnocchi piccoli. Cook for a further 5 minutes, stirring occasionally. Serve garnished with fresh oregano sprigs.

Pasta with Pepper Sauce and Olives

This low-fat Pepper Sauce helps to keep the calories in this dish down. As long as the pasta used is dairy-free, this dish is also suitable for vegans.

SERVES 4

4½ cups dried rigatoni (short tubes)

dash of olive oil

⅓ cup pitted black olives, roughly chopped

grated Cheddar cheese, to serve

FOR THE PEPPER SAUCE:

2 red peppers, skinned, deseeded, and roughly chopped

4 cloves of garlic, peeled

1¼ cups vegetable broth

salt and freshly ground black pepper

Bring a large saucepan of water to the boil, and add the rigatoni with a dash of olive oil. Cook for about 10 minutes, stirring occasionally, until tender. Drain and return to the saucepan. Set aside.

To make the sauce, place the chopped pepper, garlic and vegetable broth in a food processor or blender, and season with salt and freshly ground black pepper. Purée until smooth.

Stir the Pepper Sauce into the rigatoni with the chopped olives. Serve with grated Cheddar cheese.

Tortellini, Peppers, and Pine Nut Salad

Red peppers can be used instead of chili peppers, if you prefer. For best results, allow the salad to chill for at least an hour before serving.

SERVES 4–6

scant ¾lb fresh tortellini

dash of olive oil

1 onion, very finely sliced

1 green pepper, deseeded and very finely diced

⅔ cup toasted pine nuts

1 red chili pepper, deseeded and sliced (optional)

4-inch piece of cucumber, very thinly sliced

1 orange, peeled and very thinly sliced

FOR THE DRESSING:

4 tbsp olive oil

2 tbsp sweet soya sauce

2 tbsp vinegar

salt and freshly ground black pepper

Bring a large saucepan of water to the boil, and add the tortellini with a dash of olive oil. Cook for about 4 minutes, stirring occasionally, until tender. Drain and rinse under cold running water. Drain again and set aside.

Place the tortellini in a large mixing bowl and add the remaining salad ingredients. Toss together lightly.

To make the salad dressing, place the ingredients in a screw-top jar and shake well to combine. Pour the dressing over the salad, toss, and serve.

CHILIES

Rigatoni with Peppers and Garlic

The raw garlic added at the end of the recipe gives this dish the true taste of the Mediterranean.

YELLOW

SERVES 4

¾lb dried rigatoni (large tubes)

dash of olive oil, plus 4 tbsp

1 large onion, chopped

4 cloves of garlic, finely chopped

2 large red peppers, deseeded and roughly chopped

2 large yellow peppers, deseeded and roughly chopped

2 tsp chopped, fresh thyme

salt and freshly ground black pepper

Bring a large saucepan of water to the boil, and add the rigatoni with a dash of olive oil. Cook for about 10 minutes, stirring occasionally, until tender. Drain and set aside.

Heat the remaining oil in a large frying pan. Add the onion, 2 cloves of garlic, peppers, and thyme. Cook over a medium heat for 10–15 minutes, stirring occasionally, until the vegetables are tender and beginning to brown.

Add the pasta shapes to the pepper mixture. Stir in the remaining garlic and seasoning. Serve immediately.

Tortellini, Peppers, and Pine Nut Salad.

Pimento Pasta

A quick store-cupboard recipe for a last-minute supper surprise.

SERVES 4

¾lb dried spaghettini

dash of olive oil, plus 2 tbsp

2 cloves of garlic, crushed

14oz can red pimento, thinly sliced

salt and freshly ground black pepper

freshly grated Parmesan cheese, to serve (optional)

Bring a large saucepan of water to the boil, and add the spaghettini with a dash of olive oil. Cook for about 10 minutes, stirring occasionally, until tender. Drain and return to the saucepan. Set aside, covered, to keep warm.

Heat the remaining olive oil in a frying pan, and add the garlic and sliced pimento. Stir-fry for 3–5 minutes, then tip into the warm spaghettini. Stir to combine. Serve with a little freshly grated Parmesan cheese, if desired.

Pasta with Green Peppers and Pesto ✓

If linguini is unavailable, spaghettini or tagliatelle will work just as well in this dish.

TARRAGON

SERVES 4

1lb fresh linguini (thin, flat strips)

dash of olive oil, plus 2 tbsp

2 cloves of garlic, crushed

½ quantity Pesto Sauce (page 10)

¼ cup vegetable broth

1 green pepper, deseeded and very thinly sliced

fresh herbs, to garnish

Bring a large saucepan of water to the boil, and add the linguini with a dash of olive oil. Cook for about 4 minutes, stirring occasionally, until tender. Drain and return to the saucepan. Stir in a dash more olive oil and set aside, covered, to keep warm.

Heat the remaining olive oil in a large frying pan and sauté the garlic for 1–2 minutes, then stir in the Pesto Sauce. Add the vegetable broth, stir, and cook for 1 minute, then add the pepper slices. Cook for a further 7–10 minutes, stirring occasionally, until the pepper has softened. Stir the pepper mixture into the linguini and serve, garnished with fresh herbs.

Minty Pepper Salad

Serve this cool, light, and refreshing salad for a summer lunch, or make it for a picnic since it packs and travels well.

3¼ cups dried macaroni

dash of olive oil, plus extra for drizzling

1 yellow pepper, deseeded and cut into
½-inch diamonds

1 green pepper, deseeded and cut into
½-inch diamonds

14oz can artichoke hearts, drained and
quartered

6-inch piece of cucumber, sliced

handful of mint leaves

salt and freshly ground black pepper

1⅓ cups freshly grated Parmesan cheese

Bring a large saucepan of water to the boil, and add the macaroni with a dash of olive oil. Cook for about 10 minutes, stirring occasionally, until tender. Drain, and rinse under cold running water. Drain again, then place in a large mixing bowl.

Add the remaining ingredients to the pasta and mix well to combine. Drizzle some olive oil over the salad, then serve.

YELLOW

√ # Red Pepper Soup

This delicious, wholesome, filling soup can be served with your favorite pasta shapes.

SERVES 4

14oz can pimento, drained

2½ cups vegetable broth

salt and freshly ground black pepper

1 tbsp ground coriander

½lb cooked pasta shapes, such as tortelloni, shells, bows, etc

fresh coriander, to garnish

Place the pimento in a food processor or blender, and purée until smooth. Transfer to a large saucepan and add the vegetable broth, salt and pepper, and ground coriander. Stir and cook over gentle heat for about 10 minutes. Add the cooked pasta shapes and cook for a further 2–3 minutes, until heated through. Serve garnished with fresh coriander.

Sweet and Sour Peppers

Quick and easy, this dish makes an excellent appetizer or main course, and can be served either warm or cold.

SERVES 4–6

4 cups dried farfalle (bows)

dash of olive oil, plus 4 tbsp

2 onions, sliced

2 cloves of garlic, crushed

1½lb black peppers, deseeded and cut into chunks

1 red pepper, deseeded and cut into strips

3 packed tbsp soft brown sugar

scant ¼ cup raisins

juice of 2 lemons

⅔ cup vegetable broth

salt and freshly ground black pepper

chopped, fresh parsley, to garnish

Bring a large saucepan of water to the boil, and add the farfalle with a dash of olive oil. Cook for about 10 minutes, stirring occasionally, until tender. Drain and set aside.

Heat the remaining olive oil in a large frying pan, and add the onion and garlic. Sauté for about 3 minutes, until the onion has softened.

Add the black and red peppers. Stir, cover, and cook over gentle heat for about 10 minutes, stirring occasionally, until the peppers have softened.

Stir in the remaining ingredients and simmer, uncovered, for about 5 minutes, stirring occasionally, until the sauce has reduced slightly.

Add the cooked farfalle, and stir well to combine. Serve sprinkled with chopped fresh parsley.

Red Pepper Soup

Fusilli with Roasted Peppers.

Fusilli with Roasted Peppers ✓

To prevent the pasta from sticking together, wash off the starchy cooking liquid by rinsing the pasta under boiling water from the kettle. Continue as directed in the recipe.

SERVES 4–6

1lb dried long fusilli

dash of olive oil

2 yellow peppers, deseeded and cut into chunks

3 cloves of garlic, crushed

¼ cup olive oil

1½ cups grated Cheddar cheese

⅔ cup freshly grated Parmesan cheese

chopped, fresh parsley, to garnish

Bring a large saucepan of water to the boil, and add the fusilli with a dash of olive oil. Cook for about 10 minutes, stirring occasionally, until tender. Drain, return to the saucepan, and set aside.

Arrange the chunks of pepper on a baking sheet, and place in the broiler for about 5 minutes, or until slightly charred. Preheat the oven to 400°F.

Mix the pepper into the pasta with the remaining ingredients, and toss together to combine. Transfer to an ovenproof dish and bake for about 15 minutes, or until heated through and the cheese has melted. Sprinkle with the chopped parsley, and serve.

Cheesy Pepper Supper

Based on the traditional macaroni and cheese, this colorful, tasty supper is a great dish for kids.

YELLOW

SERVES 4–6

2¼ cups dried macaroni

½ red pepper, deseeded and finely diced

½ yellow pepper, deseeded and finely diced

dash of olive oil

FOR THE SAUCE:

¼ cup butter

½ cup all-purpose flour

2½ cups milk

2 tsp French mustard

scant ½ cup grated Cheddar cheese

salt and freshly ground black pepper

FOR THE TOPPING:

1 cup fresh breadcrumbs

¾ cup grated Cheddar cheese

Bring a large saucepan of water to the boil, and add the macaroni with the diced peppers and a dash of olive oil. Cook for about 10 minutes, stirring occasionally, until tender. Drain and transfer to a shallow, ovenproof dish. Set aside. Preheat the oven to 400°F.

To make the sauce, melt the butter in a large saucepan, then stir in the flour to make a paste. Gradually stir in the milk, a little at a time, until evenly blended, with no lumps.

Gently bring the sauce to the boil, stirring constantly, until thickened. Stir in the mustard and cheese and season with salt and pepper. Continue to cook for a further 1–2 minutes, until the cheese has melted.

Pour the cheese sauce over the macaroni and pepper mixture, and mix it in with a spoon. When the sauce and pasta are evenly combined, sprinkle with the topping ingredients and bake for 25–30 minutes, until crisp and golden.

Tricolored Purée with Pasta

This dinner-party dish can be prepared the day before and kept in the fridge. Reheat the sauces just before serving.

1lb dried spaghetti

dash of olive oil

¼ cup butter

1⅓ cups freshly grated Parmesan cheese

salt and freshly ground black pepper

FOR THE SAUCES:

3 red peppers, deseeded and chopped

2 green peppers, deseeded and chopped

1 yellow pepper, deseeded and chopped

3¾ cups vegetable broth

2 tsp tomato paste

1 tbsp chopped, fresh parsley

½ tsp ground turmeric

salt and freshly ground black pepper

Bring a large saucepan of water to the boil, and add the spaghetti with a dash of olive oil. Cook for about 10 minutes, stirring occasionally, until tender. Drain and return to the saucepan. Stir in the butter and Parmesan cheese, and season with salt and freshly ground black pepper. Cover to keep warm, and set aside.

To make the sauces, place the red, green, and yellow peppers in a large saucepan and cover with boiling water. Cook for about 10 minutes, then drain.

Purée each of the colors separately in a blender or food processor, washing out between colors. Place each color of pepper purée in a mixing bowl, and stir in enough vegetable broth to make the red pepper sauce up to 2½ cups, the green pepper sauce up to a scant 2 cups, and the yellow pepper sauce up to 1¼ cups.

Stir in the tomato paste into the red pepper sauce, the chopped parsley into the green pepper sauce, and the ground turmeric into the yellow pepper sauce. Season all three sauces with salt and freshly ground black pepper.

Transfer the sauces into separate saucepans to reheat, if necessary, then serve with the cheesy spaghetti.

PARSLEY

Pepper Pasta Soufflé

Perfect for a romantic dinner for two. But remember, timing is crucial! Make sure all your guests are seated before removing the soufflé from the oven.

YELLOW

SERVES 2

¼lb fresh spinach tagliatelle

dash of olive oil, plus 2 tbsp

1 clove of garlic, crushed

½lb mixed colored peppers, deseeded and cut into thin strips

2 tbsp chopped, fresh oregano

FOR THE SOUFFLÉ:

3 tbsp butter, plus extra for greasing

4 level tbsp all-purpose flour

1½ cups milk

⅓ cup freshly grated Parmesan cheese

4 eggs, separated

Bring a large saucepan of water to the boil, and add the tagliatelle with a dash of olive oil. Cook for 3–5 minutes, stirring occasionally, until tender. Drain and roughly chop. Set aside.

Heat the remaining olive oil in a frying pan, and add the garlic. Cook for 1–2 minutes, then stir in the pepper strips with the oregano. Cover and cook over gentle heat for about 10 minutes, stirring occasionally, until the peppers have softened. Remove from the heat and set aside. Preheat the oven to 400°F.

To make the soufflé, butter two small soufflé dishes and set aside. Melt the butter in a saucepan, and stir in the flour to make a paste. Gradually stir in the milk, then bring the sauce to the boil, stirring constantly to prevent lumps, until thickened.

Stir in the Parmesan cheese and beat in the egg yolks, one at a time. Stir in the chopped tagliatelle until evenly coated.

Whisk the egg whites in a clean, dry bowl until stiff. Fold the egg whites into the tagliatelle mixture, then divide between the prepared soufflé dishes. Spoon the pepper mixture on top of each soufflé, then bake for 20–25 minutes until risen and golden. Serve immediately.

4 **Pasta** *with Brassicas*

✓ Floret Soup

A pretty and delicately flavored soup for a dinner-party menu. Make it in advance and reheat to serve.

SERVES 4–6

2 tbsp butter

2 cloves of garlic, crushed

¾lb tiny broccoli, cauliflower, and romanesco florets

½ cup dried pastina (any tiny shapes)

5 cups vegetable broth

salt and freshly ground black pepper

Melt the butter in a large saucepan, and sauté the garlic for about 2 minutes. Add the tiny florets to the garlic and cook for about 5 minutes, stirring occasionally, until tender.

Stir the pastina into the floret mixture, cook for 1–2 minutes, then add the vegetable broth. Season with salt and freshly ground black pepper, cover, and bring to the boil. Simmer for about 10 minutes, until the pastina is cooked and the florets have softened. Serve with warm, fresh bread.

Baby Cauliflower and Broccoli Cheese

Baby vegetables can be both formal and fun. To make this recipe suitable for children, omit the wine and cream from the sauce.

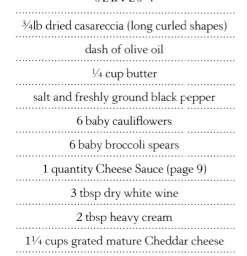

BROCCOLI

SERVES 4

¾lb dried casareccia (long curled shapes)

dash of olive oil

¼ cup butter

salt and freshly ground black pepper

6 baby cauliflowers

6 baby broccoli spears

1 quantity Cheese Sauce (page 9)

3 tbsp dry white wine

2 tbsp heavy cream

1¼ cups grated mature Cheddar cheese

Bring a large saucepan of water to the boil, and add the casareccia with a dash of olive oil. Cook for about 10 minutes, stirring occasionally, until tender. Drain and return to the saucepan with the butter, and season with salt and freshly ground black pepper. Set aside, covered, to keep warm.

Bring a large saucepan of water to the boil, and add the baby cauliflower and baby broccoli. Cook for about 5 minutes, until tender. Drain and return to the saucepan, covered, to keep warm.

Place the Cheese Sauce in a saucepan, and stir in the wine and cream. Heat gently, stirring constantly, for about 5 minutes.

To serve, divide the pasta between four warmed individual plates and arrange the baby vegetables on top. Pour the Cheese Sauce over the pasta, and sprinkle with grated cheese. Serve immediately.

Gnocchetti Sardi with Broccoli and Tomatoes

A lovely light lunch or supper dish. Choose vivid green, tightly packed heads of broccoli, and cook as briefly as possible to retain the color and crisp texture.

TARRAGON

SERVES 4

¾lb dried gnocchetti sardi (small dumpling shapes)

dash of olive oil

⅓ cup unsalted butter

¾lb small broccoli florets

1 clove of garlic, chopped

2 tsp chopped, fresh rosemary

2 tsp chopped, fresh oregano

salt and freshly ground black pepper

7oz can chopped tomatoes

1 tbsp tomato paste

fresh herbs, to garnish

Bring a large saucepan of water to the boil, and add the gnocchetti sardi with a dash of olive oil. Cook for about 6 minutes, stirring occasionally, until tender. Drain and return to the saucepan, covered, to keep warm.

Meanwhile, melt the butter in a large frying pan. Add the broccoli, garlic, rosemary and oregano, and season with salt and freshly ground black pepper. Cover and cook gently for about 5 minutes, until tender.

Add the chopped tomatoes and tomato paste, and stir. Add the gnocchetti sardi, mix together lightly, then serve immediately, garnished with fresh herbs.

Buckwheat Noodles with Savoy Cabbage

Buckwheat noodles, known as "pizzoccheri," are a specialty of northern Italy, and are available from some Italian delicatessens. Wholewheat or egg tagliatelle make good substitutes.

SERVES 6

¾lb dried buckwheat noodles

½lb savoy cabbage, shredded

1 medium potato, peeled and diced

dash of olive oil

½ cup plus 2 tbsp unsalted butter

2 cloves of garlic, chopped

4 tbsp chopped, fresh sage

pinch of freshly grated nutmeg

scant ½lb diced Fontina cheese

1⅓ cups freshly grated Parmesan cheese

Bring a large saucepan of water to the boil, and add the buckwheat noodles, cabbage, and potato with a dash of olive oil. Cook for 10–15 minutes, stirring occasionally, until tender. Drain and set aside, covered, to keep warm.

Meanwhile, melt the butter in a large frying pan, and sauté the garlic and sage for about 1 minute. Remove from the heat and set aside.

Place a layer of the pasta and vegetables in a warm serving dish, and sprinkle with a little nutmeg, some of the Fontina cheese, and some of the Parmesan cheese.

Repeat the layers, then pour the hot garlic butter over the pasta. Mix lightly into the pasta and serve immediately.

Gnocchetti Sardi with Broccoli and Tomatoes.

Braised Red Cabbage and Pasta Bake

This hearty supper dish for the family is delicious teamed with mashed potatoes.

½lb dried ziti (short macaroni)

dash of olive oil

¼ cup butter

1 onion, chopped

2 cloves of garlic, crushed

1 tbsp chopped, fresh thyme

1lb red cabbage, chopped

⅔ cup sultanas

scant ½ cup roasted pine nuts

salt and freshly ground black pepper

2¼ cups grated mature Cheddar cheese

Bring a large saucepan of water to the boil, and add the ziti with a dash of olive oil. Cook for about 10 minutes, stirring occasionally, until tender. Drain and set aside. Preheat the oven to 400°F.

Melt the butter in a large frying pan, and sauté the onion, garlic, and thyme for about 3 minutes, until softened. Add the chopped red cabbage, sultanas and pine nuts, and season to taste with salt and freshly ground black pepper. Cover and cook for 10 minutes, stirring occasionally, until the cabbage has softened.

Stir in the ziti, then transfer the mixture to a shallow, ovenproof dish. Top with the grated Cheddar cheese and bake for about 20 minutes, until golden. Serve immediately.

FUSILLI

Cheesy Cauliflower Crumble

A great way of serving vegetables as a main course. Serve this crumble with lightly cooked green beans and mashed potatoes for a really satisfying family supper.

SERVES 4

⅓ cup dried pastina (any tiny shapes)

dash of olive oil

2lb cauliflower florets, trimmed

¼ cup butter

salt and freshly ground black pepper

FOR THE TOPPING:

1 generous cup rolled oats

1 cup ground hazelnuts

1 cup ground almonds

1 small onion, very finely chopped

1 clove of garlic, crushed

1 tsp dried thyme

salt and freshly ground black pepper

¼ cup butter

¾ cup grated mature Cheddar cheese

Bring a large saucepan of water to the boil, and add the pastina with a dash of olive oil. Cook for about 8 minutes, stirring occasionally, until tender. Drain, and rinse under cold running water. Drain again.

Place the cauliflower florets in a large saucepan of boiling water and cook for 10–15 minutes, until tender. Drain, reserving the cooking water, and return to the saucepan. Place about a third of the cauliflower and ¼ cup butter in a food processor or blender with enough of the reserved cooking water to make a smooth purée. Stir the cauliflower purée into the remaining florets, and season with salt and pepper. Transfer the cauliflower mixture to a shallow, ovenproof dish and set aside. Preheat the oven to 350°F.

To make the topping, place the pastina in a mixing bowl with the rolled oats, ground nuts, onion, garlic, and dried thyme. Season with salt and freshly ground black pepper and rub in ¼ cup butter until the mixture resembles coarse breadcrumbs.

Sprinkle the topping over the cauliflower mixture, then scatter the grated cheese on top. Bake for about 35 minutes, until crisp and golden.

RED CABBAGE

Cabbage and Pasta Mold.

Cabbage and Pasta Mold

Serve as an impressive dish for family or friends. Quick and easy to prepare, your guests will certainly be impressed.

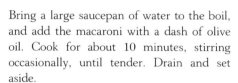

SERVES 4–6

1¾ cups dried wholewheat macaroni

dash of olive oil, plus extra for greasing

½lb small cauliflower florets

1¼ cups Tomato Sauce (page 9)

4 tbsp freshly grated Parmesan cheese

¾ cup grated mature Cheddar cheese

2 tbsp chopped, fresh parsley

salt and freshly ground black pepper

5 large savoy cabbage leaves, stalks removed

fresh herbs, to garnish

Bring a large saucepan of water to the boil, and add the macaroni with a dash of olive oil. Cook for about 10 minutes, stirring occasionally, until tender. Drain and set aside.

Meanwhile, blanch the cauliflower florets in boiling water, drain, and place in a bowl.

Stir in the macaroni, Parmesan and Cheddar cheeses, the Tomato Sauce, and chopped parsley, then season with salt and freshly ground black pepper. Allow to cool completely.

Preheat the oven to 350°F. Blanch the cabbage leaves in boiling water, then drain and rinse under cold running water immediately. Pat dry with paper towels, then use to line a greased, ovenproof bowl, overlapping the leaves and covering the base. Allow the leaves to hang over the sides of the bowl.

Spoon the cool pasta mixture into the prepared bowl, pressing down firmly with the back of the spoon. Fold the overhanging leaves over the top to encase the pasta filling. Cover the top of the bowl with greased aluminum foil, and bake in the center of the oven for about 25–30 minutes. Leave to stand for 10 minutes before inverting onto a serving plate. Garnish with fresh herbs, and serve.

Brassicas with Bavettini

This is a good store-cupboard recipe as any of the brassica family work well here. You could also vary the type of pasta used, according to what you have in your cupboard.

SERVES 4–6

1lb dried bavettini (long, thin, flat shapes)

dash of olive oil, plus 3 tbsp

3 cloves of garlic, crushed

1 onion, finely chopped

3 tbsp chopped, fresh rosemary

¾lb mixed brassicas, such as broccoli, cauliflower, kale and cabbage, chopped or shredded

salt and freshly ground black pepper

extra olive oil and freshly grated Parmesan cheese, to serve

Bring a large saucepan of water to the boil, and add the bavettini with a dash of olive oil. Cook for about 10 minutes, stirring occasionally, until tender. Drain and set aside.

Heat the olive oil in a large frying pan and sauté the garlic, onion, and rosemary for about 3 minutes, until the onion has softened.

Add the chopped or shredded brassicas, and season with salt and freshly ground black pepper. Cook for about 10 minutes, until the vegetables are tender.

Toss in the cooked bavettini and cook for about 3 minutes, stirring frequently, until the brassicas have mixed in and the dish is heated through.

Serve drizzled with extra olive oil and sprinkled with freshly grated Parmesan.

✓ Chinese Mustard Greens with Fusilli

This quick-to-prepare, nutritious dish is perfect for a light lunch when entertaining friends.

SERVES 4–6

3½ cups dried fusilli (small twists)

dash of olive oil

3 tbsp sesame oil

3 cloves of garlic, crushed

2 carrots, peeled and cut into ribbons

8 scallions, stalks removed and leaves shredded

5–6 tbsp dark soya sauce

3 tbsp toasted sesame seeds

Bring a large saucepan of water to the boil, and add the fusilli with a dash of olive oil. Cook for about 10 minutes, stirring occasionally, until the pasta is tender. Drain thoroughly, and set aside.

Heat the sesame oil in a wok or large frying pan, and add the garlic. Stir-fry for 30 seconds, then add the carrot ribbons. Continue to cook for 3–4 minutes, then add the shredded scallions. Cook for 2–3 minutes, stirring continuously.

Stir in the soya sauce, sesame seeds, and the fusilli. Cook for a further 2 minutes, and serve immediately.

> **TIP:**
> To cut the carrots into wafer-thin ribbons, peel away the outside skin using a vegetable peeler, then continue peeling the carrot.

FUSILLI

Stilton and Broccoli Soup with Tortelloni ✓

A meal in itself, this recipe provides all the richness, flavor, and hunger satisfaction your guests could possibly require.

SERVES 4–6

½lb fresh tortelloni (choose your favorite filling)

dash of olive oil

¼ cup butter

1 clove of garlic, crushed

1lb broccoli spears, trimmed

5 cups vegetable broth

¼lb Stilton cheese, crumbled

salt and freshly ground black pepper

5 tbsp light cream

Bring a large saucepan of water to the boil, and add the tortelloni with a dash of olive oil. Cook for about 5 minutes, stirring occasionally, until tender. Drain and set aside.

Melt the butter in a large saucepan, and sauté the garlic for about 2 minutes. Add the broccoli spears and continue to cook for about 5 minutes, stirring frequently.

Add the vegetable broth to the broccoli mixture, and gradually bring the soup to the boil. Simmer for about 5 minutes, until the broccoli has softened. Purée the soup, in batches if necessary, in a food processor or blender until smooth.

Return the soup to the cleaned saucepan, and place over gentle heat. Stir in the crumbled Stilton cheese, and season with salt and freshly ground black pepper. Cook for about 3 minutes, until the cheese has melted. Stir in the cream and tortelloni. Cook for 2–3 minutes to heat through, then serve immediately.

BROCCOLI

Pasta-stuffed Cabbage Leaves

Easy to prepare and sure to impress the guests, this dish can be made the day before and kept in the refrigerator. Allow an extra 15–20 minutes to reheat in the oven before serving.

TORTELLINI

SERVES 4

½ cup dried gnocchetti sardi (dumpling shapes) and/or pastina (any tiny shapes)

dash of olive oil

8 large savoy cabbage leaves, stalks removed

FOR THE FILLING:

2 tbsp olive oil

2 cloves of garlic, crushed

2 carrots, peeled and grated

2 zucchini, grated

4 tomatoes, skinned, deseeded, and chopped

½ cup chopped walnuts

salt and freshly ground black pepper

FOR THE SAUCE:

14oz can chopped tomatoes

4 tbsp dry red wine

⅔ cup vegetable broth

1 tbsp dried oregano

1 onion, very finely chopped

salt and freshly ground black pepper

Bring a large saucepan of water to the boil, and add the pasta with a dash of olive oil. Cook for about 10 minutes, stirring occasionally, until tender. Drain and set aside.

Blanch the cabbage leaves in boiling water, then quickly immerse in cold water and drain. Pat dry with paper towels, and set aside.

To make the filling, heat the olive oil in a large frying pan and sauté the garlic for about 1 minute. Add the grated carrots and zucchini, and cook for a further 3–4 minutes, stirring occasionally, until tender.

Add the chopped tomatoes, walnuts, and pasta. Season with salt and freshly ground black pepper. Cook for about 5 minutes, stirring occasionally, then set aside to cool.

To make the sauce, place all the ingredients in a saucepan and bring to simmering point. Cook for 20–30 minutes, stirring occasionally, until reduced and thickened. Allow to cool slightly, then transfer to a food processor or blender and purée until smooth. Set aside. Preheat the oven to 400°F.

To assemble the stuffed cabbage leaves, lay the blanched leaves out on the work surface, concave side uppermost, and divide the mixture between the leaves, placing it in the center of each. Fold the edges of each leaf over to completely encase the filling, securing with a toothpick.

Arrange the stuffed leaves in a shallow ovenproof dish, and pour the sauce around the edges. Cover with aluminum foil and bake for about 20 minutes, until heated through. Serve immediately, with any extra sauce served separately.

Lasagnette with Cauliflower and Broccoli

Ask for "mature Pecorino"
or "Pecorino Sardo,"
which are hard cheeses.
Alternatively, use
Parmesan cheese.

SERVES 6

¾lb dried plain and tomato lasagnette
(ruffle-edged ribbons)

dash of olive oil, plus ¼ cup

½lb small cauliflower florets

½lb small broccoli florets

2 cloves of garlic, crushed

1 cup freshly grated Pecorino cheese

pinch of freshly grated nutmeg

2 tbsp chopped, fresh parsley

salt and freshly ground black pepper

Bring a large saucepan of water to the boil, and add the lasagnette with a dash of olive oil. Cook for about 10 minutes, stirring occasionally until tender. Drain and set aside, covered.

Bring two saucepans of water to the boil, and add the cauliflower and broccoli florets. Cook for about 8–10 minutes, until tender. Drain and set aside.

Heat the olive oil in a frying pan, and sauté the garlic for about 1 minute. Add the cauliflower, broccoli, lasagnette, about two-thirds of the Pecorino cheese, nutmeg and parsley, and season with salt and freshly ground black pepper. Mix well, then transfer to a warm serving dish and sprinkle with the remaining Pecorino cheese. Serve immediately.

Spaghetti with Cauliflower Sauce

A cheesy change from the more traditional spaghetti sauces, this one will definitely have them coming back for more!

SERVES 4–6

1lb dried spaghetti

dash of olive oil

2 tbsp butter

⅓ cup freshly grated Parmesan cheese

freshly ground black pepper

FOR THE SAUCE:

¼ cup butter

2 cloves of garlic, crushed

3 tbsp chopped, fresh parsley

¾lb cauliflower florets, finely chopped

½ cup all-purpose flour

1¼ cups vegetable broth

1¼ cups milk

salt and freshly ground black pepper

2 cups grated mature Cheddar cheese, plus extra, to serve

Bring a large saucepan of water to the boil, and add the spaghetti with a dash of olive oil. Cook for about 10 minutes, stirring occasionally, until tender. Drain and return to the saucepan. Toss in the butter and Parmesan cheese. Season with freshly ground black pepper, then set aside, covered, to keep warm.

Melt the butter in a large saucepan and sauté the garlic and parsley for about 2 minutes, then add the cauliflower florets. Stir, cover, and cook for about 8 minutes, until the cauliflower has softened slightly.

Stir in the flour, then gradually stir in the vegetable broth and the milk, stirring well after each addition to prevent any lumps.

Slowly bring the sauce to boiling point, stirring constantly, until thickened. Season with salt and freshly ground black pepper, and stir in the grated Cheddar cheese. Cook for a further 2–3 minutes, stirring, until the cheese has melted. Serve the spaghetti on warmed individual plates with the cauliflower sauce, sprinkled with a little extra grated Cheddar cheese.

Cannelloni with Greens and Walnuts

Serve with a simple, crisp, fresh salad to complement the rich, cheesy sauce and walnut filling. Fresh spinach is a good alternative for this recipe.

SERVES 4

12 dried cannelloni (tubes)

dash of olive oil

butter, for greasing

½ cup walnuts, chopped

FOR THE FILLING:

3 tbsp olive oil

1 large onion, chopped

1 clove of garlic, crushed

1lb mustard greens, shredded

7oz can chopped tomatoes

1 tsp dried oregano

3 tbsp chopped, fresh basil

½lb ricotta cheese

1 cup fresh whole-wheat breadcrumbs

½ cup walnuts

good pinch of freshly grated nutmeg

salt and freshly ground black pepper

FOR THE CHEESE SAUCE:

2 tbsp butter

¼ cup all-purpose flour

1¼ cups milk

⅔ cup grated Fontina cheese

Bring a large saucepan of water to the boil, and add the cannelloni with a dash of olive oil. Cook for about 10 minutes, stirring occasionally, until tender. Drain and rinse under cold running water. Drain again, then pat dry with paper towels and set aside.

BASIL

To make the filling, heat the olive oil in a large frying pan and sauté the onion and garlic for 2–3 minutes, until the onion has softened. Add the mustard greens, tomatoes, and oregano. Continue to cook for about 5 minutes, stirring frequently, until the liquid has completely evaporated. Remove from the heat and leave to cool.

Place the mustard greens mixture in a food processor or blender, and add the basil, ricotta cheese, breadcrumbs, walnuts, and nutmeg. Purée until smooth, then season with salt and freshly ground black pepper.

To make the sauce, melt the butter in a saucepan. Stir in the flour and cook for 1 minute. Gradually stir in the milk, and heat until bubbling and thickened. Stir in the grated Fontina cheese.

Preheat the oven to 375°F. Butter the insides of a shallow, ovenproof dish. Using a teaspoon, stuff each cannelloni with the filling, then lay it in the dish.

Pour the cheese sauce evenly over the cannelloni. Sprinkle with walnuts and bake for about 30 minutes, until bubbling and golden.

TIP:

Sheets of fresh lasagne can be used instead of dried cannelloni. Make up ½ quantity Pasta Dough (page 8), and roll out to ¼ inch thick. Cut into 4 × 6 inch rectangles, and spoon some of the filling along the short end of the sheet of pasta. Roll it up into a neat tube, and place in the dish with the sealed end underneath.

Sprout Soup with Almonds

A warming soup with a subtle flavor, this makes an excellent starter for a dinner party. Made up to two days in advance, this soup can be reheated just before serving.

SERVES 4–6

¼ cup butter

1 clove of garlic, crushed

2 tsp chopped, fresh rosemary

½lb Brussels sprouts, finely shredded

1¼ cups dried ditalini rigati (tiny, short, ridged tubes)

scant ½ cup toasted, flaked almonds

6½ cups vegetable broth

salt and freshly ground black pepper

4 tbsp light cream

freshly grated Parmesan cheese, to serve

Melt the butter in a large saucepan, and sauté the garlic and rosemary for about 2 minutes. Add the shredded Brussels sprouts and cook for a further 3–4 minutes, stirring occasionally. Add the ditalini rigati with the flaked almonds. Stir and cook for 1–2 minutes, then stir in the vegetable broth and season with salt and freshly ground black pepper.

Cover the soup and simmer for about 10 minutes, stirring occasionally. Stir in the cream, then serve in individual bowls with freshly grated Parmesan cheese.

BRUSSELS SPROUTS

5 **Pasta** *with Various Vegetables*

Vegetable and Fresh Coriander Soup

A light, fresh-tasting soup
that is ideal either as an
appetizer or as a light
lunch.

5 cups vegetable broth

1¾ cups dried pasta (any shape)

dash of olive oil

2 carrots, thinly sliced

1½ cups frozen peas

6 tbsp chopped, fresh coriander

salt and freshly ground black pepper

Bring the vegetable broth to the boil in a
large saucepan, and add the pasta with a
dash of olive oil. Cook for about 5 minutes,
stirring occasionally, then add the sliced
carrots.

Cook for 5 minutes, then add the peas
and coriander. Season with salt and freshly
ground black pepper and simmer gently for
about 10 minutes, stirring occasionally, until
the pasta and carrots are tender. Serve the
soup with finely grated cheese, if wished.

Minestrone Soup ✓

There are many different versions of this classic soup; this one is simple, wholesome, and filling. Serve with warm, crusty garlic bread.

CARROTS

SERVES 4–6

5 tbsp extra virgin olive oil

3 cloves of garlic, crushed

6 carrots, peeled and finely diced

3 medium zucchini, finely diced

⅓ cup dried pastina (any tiny pasta shapes)

5 tbsp chopped, fresh parsley

2 heaped tbsp vegetable purée

6½ cups good vegetable broth

salt and freshly ground black pepper

freshly grated Parmesan cheese, to serve

Heat the olive oil in a large saucepan, and add the garlic. Sauté for about 2 minutes, then stir in the diced carrots and zucchini. Cook for about 5 minutes, stirring occasionally.

Stir the pastina and chopped parsley into the vegetable mixture, add the vegetable purée and vegetable broth, and season with salt and freshly ground black pepper.

Cover and simmer for about 30 minutes, until the vegetables and pasta have softened and the flavors have developed. Serve with freshly grated Parmesan cheese.

Pasta Paella

Based on the classic recipe, this dish makes a delicious, nutritious alternative, using pasta as the main ingredient. Any pasta shape will do; or use a combination of shapes for extra texture.

FARFALLE

1lb dried farfalle (bows)

1 tsp ground turmeric

dash of olive oil, plus 3 tbsp

2 cloves of garlic, crushed

1 Spanish onion

1 red pepper, deseeded and chopped

¼lb baby carrots

16 baby corn

¼lb snow peas

¼lb fresh asparagus tips

½ cup pitted black olives

3 level tsp flour

Bring a large saucepan of water to the boil, and add the farfalle with the ground turmeric and a dash of olive oil. Cook for about 10 minutes, stirring occasionally, until tender. Drain, reserving the cooking liquid, and set aside.

Heat the remaining olive oil in a large frying pan and sauté the garlic and onion for about 3 minutes, until softened. Add the red pepper, carrots and corn, and stir to combine. Cook for 2–3 minutes, then stir in the snow peas, asparagus tips, black olives, and farfalle. Cook for 2–3 minutes, then sprinkle with the flour and mix it into the vegetable mixture. Cook for 1 minute, then gradually stir in a little less than 2 cups of the reserved pasta cooking liquid. Cook for 2–3 minutes, until the sauce is bubbling and thickened. Serve straight from the pan, or transfer to a warmed serving dish.

ASPARAGUS

Tagliarini with Green Beans and Garlic

A delicious summer salad, hot main course or vegetable accompaniment, this dish is suitable for almost any occasion.

ROTELLE

SERVES 4–6

¾lb dried tagliarini (flat spaghetti)

dash of olive oil, plus 4 tbsp

¾lb green beans

1 medium potato, cut into ½-inch cubes

3 cloves of garlic, chopped

5 tbsp chopped, fresh sage

salt and freshly ground black pepper

freshly grated Parmesan cheese, to serve

Bring a large saucepan of water to the boil, and add the tagliarini with a dash of olive oil. Cook for about 10 minutes, stirring occasionally, until tender. Drain and set aside.

Cook the beans and potato cubes in a large saucepan of boiling water for about 10 minutes, until tender. Drain well, and set aside to keep warm.

Heat the remaining olive oil in a large frying pan, add the garlic and sage, and season with salt and freshly ground black pepper. Sauté for 2–3 minutes, then add the cooked beans and potato. Cook for 1–2 minutes, then add the cooked tagliarini and mix well.

Cook for about 5 minutes, stirring occasionally, then transfer to a warmed serving dish. Sprinkle with freshly grated Parmesan cheese and serve.

Fettuccine with Garlicky Creamed Spinach

This tasty recipe is quick and easy to prepare. Serve immediately with plenty of freshly grated Parmesan cheese.

SERVES 4–6

1lb dried fettuccine

dash of olive oil

2 tbsp butter

3 cloves of garlic, crushed

1lb frozen chopped spinach, thawed and well drained

1¼ cups light cream

pinch of freshly grated nutmeg

salt and freshly ground black pepper

⅔ cup freshly grated Parmesan cheese, plus extra to serve

Bring a large saucepan of water to the boil, and add the fettuccine with a dash of olive oil. Cook for about 8 minutes, stirring occasionally, until tender. Drain and set aside, covered, to keep warm.

Melt the butter in a large frying pan and sauté the garlic for 1–2 minutes, then add the spinach. Cook over medium heat for about 5 minutes, stirring frequently, until the moisture has evaporated.

Add the cream and nutmeg, and season with salt and freshly ground black pepper. Toss in the fettuccine and Parmesan cheese, stir, and cook for a final minute. Serve with extra freshly grated Parmesan cheese.

Stuffed Zucchini

A delicious combination of tender zucchini and fresh coriander mixed with a sweet soya sauce. You can make the filling and the sauce a day in advance. Reheat the sauce while the zucchini are baking.

SERVES 4–6

¼lb dried vermicelli (very thin spaghetti), broken into small pieces

dash of olive oil

4 medium-sized zucchini

finely chopped walnuts, to garnish

FOR THE FILLING:

⅔ cup sweet soya sauce

1 clove of garlic, crushed

½ cup mushrooms, very finely chopped

3 tbsp chopped, fresh coriander

⅓ cup shelled walnuts, very finely chopped

salt and freshly ground black pepper

FOR THE SAUCE:

4 tbsp olive oil

2 cloves of garlic, crushed

1 cup chopped, fresh coriander

salt and freshly ground black pepper

3 tbsp vegetable broth

Bring a large saucepan of water to the boil, and add the vermicelli with a dash of olive oil. Cook for about 5 minutes, stirring occasionally, until tender. Drain and set aside.

Cut a thin slice lengthways along the top of each zucchini, and chop this piece finely. Using a teaspoon, scoop out the flesh from the middle of the zucchini and chop roughly. Arrange the hollowed zucchini in a shallow, ovenproof dish and set aside. Preheat the oven to 400°F.

To make the filling, place the sweet soya sauce and the garlic in a large frying pan and heat gently. Cook for about 1 minute, then stir in the mushrooms. Cook for about 5 minutes, stirring occasionally, then add the coriander. Cook for a further 2–3 minutes, then stir in the chopped walnuts and season to taste with salt and freshly ground black pepper. Simmer for 1–2 minutes, then stir in the cooked vermicelli.

Remove from the heat and, using a teaspoon, stuff the zucchini with the filling, placing any extra around the zucchini in the dish. Cover the dish with aluminum foil and bake for 25–30 minutes, until the zucchini are tender.

Meanwhile, to make the sauce, place all the ingredients in a food processor or blender and purée until smooth. Transfer to a small saucepan, and heat gently until warm. Remove the stuffed zucchini from the oven and serve with the coriander sauce, garnished with finely chopped walnuts.

TARRAGON

Provençal Green Beans with Pasta

A delicious way to serve green beans, piping hot with freshly grated Parmesan cheese.

SERVES 4–6

2 tbsp olive oil

3 cloves of garlic, crushed

1 onion, chopped

3 tbsp chopped, fresh thyme

1lb green beans

14oz can chopped tomatoes

2 heaped tbsp tomato paste

scant 2 cups vegetable broth

²⁄₃ cup dry red wine

salt and freshly ground black pepper

1lb dried pasta (any shapes)

2 tbsp butter

freshly grated Parmesan cheese

Heat the oil in a large frying pan, and sauté the garlic and onion for about 3 minutes, until softened. Add the thyme, beans, tomatoes, tomato paste, vegetable broth and wine, season with salt and freshly ground black pepper, and stir well to combine. Cover and cook gently for 25–30 minutes, until the beans are tender. Remove the lid and cook for a further 5–8 minutes, stirring occasionally, until the sauce has thickened slightly.

Meanwhile, bring a large saucepan of water to the boil, and add the pasta with a dash of olive oil. Cook for about 10 minutes, stirring occasionally, until tender. Drain and return to the saucepan. Toss in butter and freshly ground black pepper.

Serve the beans with the hot, buttered pasta and freshly grated Parmesan cheese.

STELLETTI

Coconut Vegetables with Pasta

Make this dish a day ahead to allow the flavors to develop. Creamed coconut is available from most supermarkets and ethnic grocers.

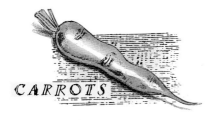

CARROTS

SERVES 4–6

3 tbsp olive oil

2 cloves of garlic, crushed

1 onion, chopped

2 tsp ground cumin

2 tsp ground coriander

½lb creamed coconut, chopped

3 cups boiling water

salt and freshly ground black pepper

1 vegetable bouillon

3 carrots, diced

2 small zucchini, diced

5 sticks celery, chopped

½ small cauliflower, separated into florets

16 baby corn

5 tbsp chopped, fresh coriander

¾lb fresh linguini (thin, flat strips)

Heat the olive oil in a large frying pan, and sauté the garlic, onion, cumin, and coriander for about 3 minutes, stirring occasionally, until the onion has softened.

Add the creamed coconut to the boiling water. Stir well, and season with salt and freshly ground black pepper. Add the bouillon cube, and stir until dissolved.

Add the vegetables and coriander to the frying pan, and stir well. Cover and simmer for 15–20 minutes, stirring occasionally, until the vegetables are tender. Remove the cover and continue to cook for about 5 minutes, until the sauce has thickened slightly.

Meanwhile, bring a large saucepan of water to the boil, and add the linguini with a dash of olive oil. Cook for about 4 minutes, stirring occasionally, until tender. Drain, and serve with the vegetables.

Pasta Baskets with Vegetables

The special piece of equipment used in this recipe is known by the French as a *nid d'oiseau*, which, loosely translated, means a "bird's nest." It is a small metal basket in a basket on long handles, commonly used to make edible baskets of potato, filo pastry, and, in this case, vermicelli.

SERVES 4

¼lb dried vermicelli

dash of olive oil

vegetable oil, for deep-frying

FOR THE FILLING:

2 tbsp sesame oil

2 cloves of garlic, crushed

16 baby corn

¼lb snow peas

2 carrots, thinly sliced

3 tbsp soya sauce

1 tbsp toasted sesame seeds

Bring a large saucepan of water to the boil, and add the vermicelli with a dash of olive oil. Cook for about 5 minutes, stirring occasionally, until tender. Drain and set aside.

Heat the oil for deep frying, and pack the cooked vermicelli into the bird's nest, if using. Otherwise, fry the vermicelli in batches in a frying basket. Cook for 3–5 minutes in hot oil, until the vermicelli is crisp and golden. Remove the basket from the bird's nest, and drain on paper towels. Repeat the process to make three more baskets. Arrange the baskets of loose vermicelli on individual serving plates. Set aside.

To make the filling, heat the sesame oil in a frying pan and sauté the garlic for 1–2 minutes. Add the corn, snow peas and carrots, stir, and cook for 3–5 minutes, until tender. Stir in the soya sauce and sprinkle with the sesame seeds. Cook for a further 2 minutes, then spoon into the vermicelli baskets or onto a bed of vermicelli to serve.

CARROTS

Pea-green Ravioli with Cheese Sauce

Fresh mint tastes a million times better than dried, so try to use it to give this dish the full flavor it deserves.

SERVES 6

⅔ quantity Pasta Dough (page 8), omitting the oil and water and adding 6 tbsp spinach liquid instead

1 quantity Cheese Sauce (page 9)

FOR THE FILLING:

2 tbsp olive oil

1 onion, very finely chopped

2 cups frozen peas

3 tbsp chopped, fresh mint

1 egg, beaten, for brushing with 2 tsp tomato paste added

dash of olive oil

fresh mint sprigs, to garnish

Keep the fresh pasta dough covered with plastic wrap at room temperature and the Cheese Sauce in a saucepan, ready to reheat.

To make the ravioli filling, heat the olive oil in a frying pan and sauté the onion for about 3 minutes, until softened. Add the frozen peas, cover and cook for about 7 minutes, stirring occasionally, until thawed and cooked through. Stir in the fresh mint, and remove from the heat. Season with salt and freshly ground black pepper.

Allow the filling mixture to cool slightly, then transfer to a blender or food processor and purée until a slightly coarse texture is achieved. Cool the mixture completely.

To make the ravioli, cut the pasta dough in half. Roll out one half to a rectangle slightly larger than 14 × 10 inches. Trim the edges of the dough neatly. Cover the rectangle with plastic wrap to prevent it drying out. Roll out the other half of the dough to the same measurements, but do not trim the edges. Cover with plastic wrap.

Place half teaspoonfuls of the filling mixture in lines, spaced about ¾ inch apart, all over the trimmed rectangle of pasta dough. Brush the beaten egg lightly in lines around the filling mixture, to make the square shapes of the ravioli.

Lay the other rectangle of dough on top and, starting at one end, seal in the filling by lightly pressing the dough, pushing out any trapped air, and gently flattening the filling to make little packets. Using a sharp knife or pastry wheel, cut down and across in lines around the filling to make the square ravioli.

To cook the ravioli, bring a large saucepan to the boil, and add the ravioli with a dash of olive oil. Cook for about 5 minutes, stirring occasionally, until tender. Drain and set aside, covered, to keep warm.

Meanwhile, reheat the Cheese Sauce over gentle heat. Serve with the cooked ravioli and garnish with fresh mint.

> **TIP:**
>
> To make 6 tbsp spinach liquid, cook ½lb fresh, chopped spinach leaves, washed and still damp, in a covered saucepan for 5 minutes, stirring frequently. Place the cooked spinach in a sieve, and press out as much green liquid as possible. Add a little extra water to make up the quantity, if necessary.

RAVIOLI

Chinese Vegetables with Pasta Noodles

Any type of pasta noodles are suitable for this recipe. Prepare them and keep them warm for only a few minutes, during which time the vegetables are quickly prepared.

SERVES 3–4

2 tbsp sesame oil

1 tsp chopped fresh ginger

2 cloves of garlic, crushed

½ cup chopped, blanched almonds

6 scallions, cut into 2-inch lengths

½lb snow peas

1 large carrot, in 2-inch lengths

1 red pepper, deseeded and cut into thin strips

1¼ cups vegetable broth

3 tbsp rich soya sauce

3 tbsp dry sherry

3 tbsp arrowroot

1½ cups beansprouts, washed and trimmed

salt and freshly ground black pepper

Heat the sesame oil in a wok or frying pan, and stir-fry the ginger and garlic for 1 minute. Stir in the chopped almonds and all the vegetables. Stir-fry for 1–2 minutes, then add the vegetable broth, soya sauce, and sherry. Mix well, and continue to cook for a further 1–2 minutes.

Mix the arrowroot in a small bowl with 1 tbsp cold water. When smooth and without lumps, stir into the vegetable mixture. Cook for 2 minutes, then add the beansprouts and season with salt and pepper. Cook for a final 1–2 minutes, until the sauce has thickened slightly. Serve with pasta noodles, cooked according to the manufacturer's instructions.

Creamy Leek and Pasta Flan

This dish is delicious both fresh out of the oven or served chilled on a hot summer's day with a crisp green salad.

SERVES 6–8

1½ cups dried orecchiette (ears)

dash of olive oil, plus 3 tbsp

a little flour, for dredging

¾lb puff pastry, thawed if frozen

2 cloves of garlic, crushed

1lb leeks, washed, trimmed, and cut into 1-inch chunks

2 tbsp chopped, fresh thyme

2 eggs, beaten

⅔ cup light cream

salt and freshly ground black pepper

1¼ cups grated Cheddar cheese

Bring a large saucepan of water to the boil, and add the orecchiette with a dash of olive oil. Cook for about 10 minutes, stirring occasionally, until tender. Drain and set aside.

Dredge the work surface with a little flour and roll out the pastry. Use to line a greased, 10-inch, loose-bottomed, fluted flan ring. Place in the refrigerator to chill for at least 10 minutes.

Preheat the oven to 375°F. Heat the remaining olive oil in a large frying pan and sauté the garlic, leeks and thyme for about 5 minutes, stirring occasionally, until tender. Stir in the orecchiette, and continue to cook for a further 2–3 minutes.

Place the beaten eggs in a small bowl, then whisk in the cream, salt, and freshly ground black pepper.

Transfer the leek and pasta mixture to the pastry case, spreading out evenly. Pour the egg and cream mixture over the top, then sprinkle with cheese. Bake for 30 minutes, until the mixture is firm and the pastry crisp.

Spinach and Mushroom Lasagne

Made in advance and put in the oven before the guests arrive, this is the perfect dish for entertaining. You can relax and enjoy the company while supper sees to itself.

SERVES 6

butter, for greasing

½lb fresh lasagne noodles

½ quantity Cheese Sauce (page 9)

⅔ cup freshly grated Parmesan cheese

FOR THE FILLING:

2 tbsp olive oil

2 cloves of garlic, crushed

1 onion, chopped

½lb mushrooms, sliced

1½lb frozen spinach, thawed and well drained

good pinch of freshly grated nutmeg

1lb cream cheese

salt and freshly ground black pepper

Make the filling first. Heat the olive oil in a large frying pan, and sauté the garlic and onion for about 3 minutes. Add the mushrooms and continue to cook for about 5 minutes, stirring occasionally. Add the spinach and nutmeg and cook for about 5 minutes, then stir in the cream cheese and season with salt and freshly ground black pepper. Cook for 3–4 minutes, until the cheese has melted and blended with the spinach mixture. Preheat the oven to 400°F.

To assemble the lasagne, butter a lasagne dish and place a layer of lasagne noodles on the bottom. Spoon some of the spinach mixture evenly over it, then add another layer of lasagne. Continue layering the pasta and spinach mixture alternately until both are used up, then pour the Cheese Sauce evenly over the top.

Sprinkle the Parmesan cheese over the lasagne and bake for about 40 minutes, until golden and bubbling.

Asparagus Ravioli with Tomato Sauce

A dinner-party dish which can be made in advance – the ravioli can even be put in the freezer several weeks before and cooked from frozen. The sauce can be made several hours ahead and reheated before serving.

SERVES 6

⅔ quantity Pasta Dough with 1 tbsp tomato paste beaten into the eggs (page 8)

1 quantity Tomato Sauce (page 9)

1 egg, beaten, for brushing

dash of olive oil

chopped fresh herbs, to garnish

FOR THE FILLING:

2 tbsp olive oil

1 clove of garlic, crushed

1 onion, very finely chopped

½lb fresh asparagus, very finely chopped

salt and freshly ground black pepper

Keep the fresh pasta dough covered with plastic wrap at room temperature, and the Tomato Sauce in a saucepan, ready to reheat before serving.

To make the filling, heat the olive oil in a frying pan and sauté the garlic and onion for about 3 minutes, until the onion has softened. Add the chopped fresh asparagus, and season with salt and freshly ground black pepper. Sauté the asparagus mixture for about 10 minutes, until softened. Set aside and allow to cool completely.

To make the ravioli, cut the pasta dough in half. Roll out one half to a rectangle slightly larger than 14 × 10 inches. Trim the edges of the dough neatly. Cover the rectangle with the plastic wrap to prevent it drying out. Roll out the other half of the dough to the same measurements. Do not trim the edges.

Place half teaspoonfuls of the filling mixture in lines, spaced about ¾ inch apart, all over the trimmed rectangle of pasta dough. Lightly brush the beaten egg in lines around the filling mixture, to make the square shapes for the ravioli.

Lay the other rectangle of pasta dough on top and, starting at one end, seal in the filling by lightly pressing the dough, pushing out any trapped air and gently flattening the filling, making little packets. Using a sharp knife or pastry wheel, cut down and then across in lines around the filling to make the square ravioli shapes.

To cook the ravioli, bring a large saucepan of water to the boil and add the ravioli with a dash of olive oil. Cook for about 6 minutes, stirring occasionally, until tender. Drain and set aside.

Meanwhile, reheat the Tomato Sauce. Serve the ravioli with the Tomato Sauce, sprinkled with chopped fresh herbs.

ASPARAGUS

Verdi Vegetables with Vermicelli

A wonderful summer dish to be eaten warm or cold, with chunks of crusty French bread.

SERVES 4–6

¾lb dried vermicelli (long, thin spaghetti)

dash of olive oil

2 tbsp butter

¾lb snow peas, sliced lengthways

2 small zucchini, shredded lengthways

½ cup pimento-stuffed olives, sliced

salt and freshly ground black pepper

2 tbsp chopped, fresh parsley

2 tbsp chopped, fresh mint

squeeze of fresh lime juice

TO GARNISH:

fresh herbs

lime slices

Bring a large saucepan of water to the boil, and add the vermicelli with a dash of olive oil. Cook for about 5 minutes, stirring occasionally, until tender. Drain and set aside.

Melt the butter in a large frying pan, and sauté the sliced snow peas and the zucchini for about 5 minutes, stirring occasionally.

Add the remaining ingredients except the lime juice to the vegetable mixture and cook for a further 5 minutes, stirring occasionally. Mix in the vermicelli and cook for 2–3 minutes, until heated through. Squeeze the fresh lime juice over the mixture and serve, garnished with fresh herbs and lime slices.

Pasta *with Pulses and Beans*

6

Lentil and Coriander Lasagne

You could make up two or three portions and freeze them uncooked. They cook beautifully from frozen at 375°F for 50–60 minutes.

SERVES 1

⅓ cup red lentils, washed and drained

1 onion, roughly chopped

2 cups boiling water

1 tbsp olive oil, plus extra for greasing

1 clove of garlic, crushed

3 tbsp chopped, fresh coriander

¼lb mushrooms, sliced

2 tsp sweet soya sauce

1 tbsp tomato paste

salt and freshly ground black pepper

1 sheet fresh lasagne (approx 8 × 4 inches), cut in half

½ quantity Cheese Sauce (page 9)

⅓ cup grated Cheddar cheese

Place the lentils and chopped onion in a large saucepan, and add the boiling water. Bring to the boil, then simmer for about 15 minutes. Drain and set aside. Preheat the oven to 400°F.

Heat the olive oil in a large frying pan and sauté the garlic and coriander for about 1 minute, then add the sliced mushrooms. Cook for about 4 minutes, then add the sweet soya sauce and tomato paste, and season with salt and freshly ground black pepper. Add the cooked lentil mixture, stir, and cook gently for about 5 minutes.

To assemble the lasagne, oil a shallow ovenproof dish and place one sheet of the lasagne on the bottom. Cover with half the lentil mixture, then add the other sheet of lasagne. Spoon the remaining lentil mixture over the top, spread out evenly, then pour the Cheese Sauce over the top. Sprinkle with grated cheese, then bake for about 20 minutes.

> **TIP:**
> This is a perfect opportunity to use up any leftover homemade pasta from another recipe – it is not worth making up a fresh batch for this dish since it uses such a small amount.

ROTELLE

Corn and Butter Bean Bake

Canned beans are ideal for this recipe, so take advantage of their convenience.

FARFALLE

SERVES 4

1 cup dried farfallini (tiny bows)

dash of olive oil

3 tbsp sunflower oil

2 cloves of garlic, crushed

1 onion, very finely chopped

3 tbsp chopped, fresh thyme

4 sticks celery, chopped

8oz can butter beans, drained

1 cup frozen corn kernels

1 tbsp wholewheat flour

1¼ cups vegetable broth

salt and freshly ground black pepper

FOR THE TOPPING:

2 tbsp sesame seeds

2 tbsp fresh wholewheat breadcrumbs

sesame oil, to drizzle

Bring a large saucepan of water to the boil, and add the farfallini with a dash of olive oil. Cook for about 8 minutes, stirring occasionally, until tender. Drain and set aside. Preheat the oven to 350°F.

Heat the sunflower oil in a large frying pan and sauté the garlic, onion, and fresh thyme for about 3 minutes, until the onion has softened.

Add the chopped celery and cook for about 3 minutes, then add the butter beans and corn. Cook for about 5 minutes, stirring occasionally, then stir in the flour until evenly blended.

Gradually stir in the vegetable broth, stirring well, then season with salt and freshly ground black pepper. Cook for about 5 minutes, then transfer the butter bean mixture to a shallow, ovenproof dish.

In a small bowl, combine the sesame seeds with the breadcrumbs, then sprinkle the mixture over the butter beans. Drizzle a little sesame oil over, then bake for about 20 minutes, until the topping is crisp. Serve immediately.

Spaghetti with Lentil Balls and Tomato Sauce

This is a great dish for the kids. Make double the amount of lentil balls and keep them, covered, in the refrigerator for several days for the kids to snack on. Serve with their favorite pasta for a fast, filling, nutritious dish.

SERVES 4–6

¾lb dried pasta (any shape)

dash of olive oil

sunflower oil, for deep-frying

14oz can chopped tomatoes

FOR THE LENTIL BALLS:

½ cup green lentils, washed and drained

¾ cup shelled walnuts or cashew nuts

1 bunch of scallions, chopped

6 tbsp dried wholewheat breadcrumbs

1 tbsp curry paste

salt and freshly ground black pepper

2 eggs, beaten

Bring a large saucepan of water to the boil, and add the pasta with a dash of olive oil. Cook for about 10 minutes, stirring occasionally, until tender. Drain, and return to the saucepan. Cover to keep warm.

To make the Lentil Balls, bring a large saucepan of water to the boil and add the lentils. Simmer for about 25 minutes, stirring occasionally, until softened. Drain well and allow to cool slightly.

Place the cooked lentils in a food processor or blender and add the nuts, scallions, breadcrumbs, curry paste, and salt and freshly ground black pepper. Purée until smooth, then gradually beat in the eggs to give a fairly firm mixture. Using slightly damp hands, roll the mixture into tiny balls and set aside on a baking sheet.

Heat the oil for deep-frying and cook the balls in batches for about 2 minutes, until crisp and cooked through. Drain on paper towels, then add to the pasta with a can of chopped tomatoes.

Place the saucepan over gentle heat to warm through, then serve immediately.

STELLETTI

Stuffed Pasta Shells

These are great as an appetizer or served as a canapé with drinks at a party. They can be made in advance and served cold, or reheated in the oven to serve warm.

BASIL

SERVES 4–6

12 dried conchiglie rigate (large shells)

dash of olive oil

FOR THE FILLING:

1¼ cups brown lentils, washed and drained

2 cloves of garlic, crushed

14oz can chopped tomatoes

1 tbsp tomato paste

3 tbsp chopped, fresh basil

¼ cup dry red wine

salt and freshly ground black pepper

FOR THE TOPPING:

4 tbsp fine dried breadcrumbs

⅓ cup finely grated fresh Parmesan cheese

3 tbsp chopped fresh parsley

Bring a large saucepan of water to the boil, and add the conchiglie rigate with a dash of olive oil. Cook for about 10 minutes, stirring occasionally, until tender. Drain, and rinse under cold running water. Drain again, and lay out on paper towels.

To make the filling, bring a large saucepan of water to the boil and add the lentils. Simmer for about 30 minutes, until tender. Drain, and rinse under boiling water.

Place the garlic, chopped tomatoes, tomato paste, fresh basil, wine, and salt and freshly ground black pepper in a large frying pan. Bring to boiling point, then reduce the heat and simmer for 2–3 minutes. Add the lentils, stir, and cook for about 10 minutes, until the moisture has evaporated and the mixture has thickened.

Use a teaspoon to stuff the pasta shells with the filling mixture, and arrange them on a baking sheet. Combine the topping ingredients in a small bowl, and sprinkle over the stuffed shells. Place in a hot broiler for about 5 minutes, until golden.

Eastern Pasta Salad

A traditional combination of mint and lemon makes this dish a salad for summer. Choose your favorite pasta shapes for this recipe, and serve with warm pitta bread to mop up the delicious dressing.

SERVES 4–6

¾lb dried pasta

dash of olive oil

14oz can chickpeas, drained

4 tbsp chopped, fresh mint

finely grated zest of 1 lemon

FOR THE DRESSING:

3 cloves of garlic, crushed

6 tbsp extra virgin olive oil

3 tbsp white wine vinegar

freshly squeezed juice of 1 lemon

salt and freshly ground black pepper

Bring a large saucepan of water to the boil, and add the pasta with a dash of olive oil. Cook for about 10 minutes, stirring occasionally, until tender. Drain and rinse under cold running water. Drain again, and place in a large mixing bowl.

Add the chickpeas, mint, and lemon zest to the pasta. Place all the dressing ingredients in a screw-top jar, and shake well to mix. Pour the dressing over the chickpea mixture and mix well to combine. Cover, and chill for at least 30 minutes. Toss before serving.

CHICK PEAS

Pasta Bean Soup

A nutritious meal in itself – low-fat and full of protein. Serve with warm, crusty garlic bread.

SERVES 4–6

2 tbsp olive oil

3 cloves of garlic, crushed

4 tbsp chopped, fresh parsley

2 cups dried wholewheat gnocchi piccoli (shells)

6½ cups vegetable broth

3 tbsp vegetable purée or tomato paste

14oz can mixed beans, such as borlotti, kidney, cannellini, etc, drained

salt and freshly ground black pepper

freshly grated Parmesan cheese, to serve

PARSLEY

Heat the olive oil in a large saucepan, and sauté the garlic with the chopped parsley for about 2 minutes. Add the gnocchi piccoli and cook for 1–2 minutes, stirring constantly.

Pour in the vegetable broth, and add the vegetable purée or tomato paste. Bring to the boil, reduce the heat, then simmer for about 10 minutes, stirring occasionally, until the pasta is tender.

Add the beans, and season with salt and freshly ground black pepper. Continue to cook for a further 5 minutes, then serve with a little freshly grated Parmesan cheese.

OPPOSITE *Pasta Bean Soup.*

Fusilli with Kidney Beans

The chili flavoring in this dish can be adjusted according to taste.

SERVES 4–6

1lb dried fusilli (short twists)

dash of olive oil

2 × 14oz cans chopped tomatoes

1 onion, sliced

3 tbsp chopped, fresh parsley

pinch of chili powder

salt and freshly ground black pepper

2 tbsp tomato paste

⅔ cup dry red wine

14oz can red kidney beans

KIDNEY BEANS

Bring a large saucepan of water to the boil, and add the fusilli with a dash of olive oil. Cook for about 10 minutes, stirring occasionally, until tender. Drain and set aside.

Place all the remaining ingredients except the kidney beans in a large frying pan, and bring to boiling point. Reduce the heat and simmer for about 10 minutes, until the liquid has reduced and the onion has softened.

Add the fusilli and kidney beans to the tomato mixture. Stir, cover, and cook for about 5 minutes, stirring occasionally. Serve immediately.

Lentil Pasta Burgers

Served with pitta bread and a little salad, these make a treat for children.

TORTELLINI

SERVES 2–4

⅓ cup dried pastina (any tiny shapes)

dash of olive oil

7oz can brown lentils, drained

4 tbsp dried wholewheat breadcrumbs

⅓ cup finely grated fresh Parmesan cheese

1 small onion, chopped

1 tbsp chopped, fresh parsley

4 tbsp crunchy peanut butter

1 tbsp tomato paste

1 tsp yeast extract

4 tbsp hot water

sunflower oil, for shallow frying

Bring a large saucepan of water to the boil, and add the pastina with a dash of olive oil. Cook for about 8 minutes, stirring occasionally, until tender. Drain, and allow to cool slightly.

Combine the pasta in a large mixing bowl with the lentils, breadcrumbs, Parmesan cheese, onion, and parsley.

Place the peanut butter, tomato paste, and yeast extract in a separate bowl and stir together with the hot water. Add this to the lentil mixture, and mix well.

Using damp hands, divide the mixture into four equal portions, and form into burger shapes. Heat the oil for shallow frying, and fry the burgers for about 5 minutes on each side. Serve hot or cold.

> **TIP:**
> The Lentil Pasta Burgers can also be broiled, if you prefer. Place on a lightly oiled baking sheet, and put in the broiler for about 3–5 minutes on each side.

Lentil and Mushroom Cannelloni

The tomato cannelloni is not essential, but adds to the attractive color of the finished dish. Dried cannelloni tubes work just as well.

SERVES 4

⅓ quantity Pasta Dough (page 8), with 1 tbsp tomato paste beaten into the eggs

dash of olive oil, plus 3 tbsp

1¼ cups brown lentils, washed and drained

3 cloves of garlic, crushed

2 tbsp dried thyme

2 × quantity Mushroom Sauce (page 9)

1¼ cups grated Cheddar cheese

chopped fresh parsley, to garnish

Roll out the pasta dough thinly to a 16-inch square, and cut it into four 4-inch wide strips. Cut the strips across to make 16 squares.

Bring a large saucepan of water to the boil, and add the squares of pasta, in batches, with a dash of olive oil. Cook for about 3 minutes, until tender. Drain, and rinse under cold running water. Pat dry with paper towels, and set aside.

Bring another large saucepan of water to the boil, and add the lentils. Cook for about 30 minutes, stirring occasionally, until tender. Drain, and rinse under boiling water. Drain again, and set aside. Preheat the oven to 350°F.

Heat the remaining olive oil in a large frying pan, and sauté the garlic and thyme for about 2 minutes. Add the lentils, stir, and cook for about 5 minutes. Remove from the heat, and set aside to cool slightly.

Place a little of the lentil mixture along one edge of each piece of pasta, and roll up to form a neat tube. Arrange the cannelloni in a shallow, ovenproof dish, seal sides down. Pour the Mushroom Sauce over the cannelloni, and sprinkle with grated cheese. Bake for about 40 minutes, until bubbling and golden. Serve garnished with chopped fresh parsley.

Bean Curry with Lasagnette

Lasagnette is a longer, thinner version of lasagne. Any form of noodles work well to serve with this recipe.

scant ¾lb lasagnette (long, thin strips with crinkled edges)

dash of olive oil, plus 2 tbsp

2 cloves of garlic, crushed

1 onion, chopped

3–4 tbsp mild curry paste

3 tbsp chopped, fresh coriander

1¼ cups vegetable broth

2 × 14oz cans mixed beans, such as black-eyed, flageolet, cannellini, etc, drained

chopped, fresh coriander

lime slices, to garnish

Bring a large saucepan of water to the boil, and add the lasagnette with a dash of olive oil. Cook for about 10 minutes, stirring occasionally, until tender. Drain, and return to the saucepan. Cover, to keep warm.

Heat the remaining olive oil in a large saucepan and sauté the garlic and onion for about 5 minutes, stirring occasionally. Stir in the curry paste, and cook for a further 2–3 minutes. Add the chopped coriander and vegetable broth, and cook for 5 minutes. Stir in the beans, cover, and cook for 10 minutes, stirring occasionally.

Serve the curry with the lasagnette, sprinkled with chopped, fresh coriander and garnished with lime slices.

FLAGEOLET BEANS

Sautéed Flageolet Beans with Fusilli

A garlicky dish, made with fresh tarragon to enhance the delicate flavors. Serve as a main course or as an accompaniment.

SERVES 2–4

3½ cups dried fusilli (short twists)

dash of olive oil, plus 4 tbsp

3 cloves of garlic, crushed

1 large onion, sliced

2 tbsp chopped, fresh tarragon

14oz can flageolet beans, drained

salt and freshly ground black pepper

Bring a large saucepan of water to the boil, and add the fusilli with a dash of olive oil. Cook for about 10 minutes, stirring occasionally, until tender. Drain and set aside.

Heat the olive oil in a large frying pan and sauté the garlic and onion for about 5 minutes, until the onion has browned slightly. Add the tarragon and beans, and season with salt and freshly ground black pepper. Cook for 2–3 minutes, then stir in the fusilli. Cook for 3–5 minutes, to heat through. Serve with a crisp green salad.

Winter Stew

You can give this vegetarian dish to carnivores – they'll never notice the lack of meat.

SERVES 4

1½ cups dried wholewheat radiatori (radiators)

dash of olive oil, plus 2 tbsp

2 cloves of garlic, crushed

1 onion, chopped

5–6 carrots, cut into ½-inch chunks

½lb button mushrooms

14oz can chopped tomatoes

2 × 14oz cans red and black kidney beans, drained

1¼ cups vegetable broth

1 tbsp paprika

2 tbsp sweet soya sauce

salt and freshly ground black pepper

1 tbsp cornstarch

Bring a large saucepan of water to the boil, and add the radiatori with a dash of olive oil. Cook for about 10 minutes, stirring occasionally, until tender. Drain and set aside.

Heat the remaining olive oil in a large saucepan and sauté the garlic and onion for about 3 minutes, stirring occasionally. Add the carrots, and cook for about 5 minutes.

Add the mushrooms and continue to cook for about 3 minutes, stirring occasionally, until slightly softened. Add the remaining ingredients, except the cornstarch, and stir in the radiatori. Cover, and cook gently for about 15 minutes, until the vegetables are tender.

In a small bowl, mix the cornstarch with a little of the cooking liquid to make a smooth paste. Add the cornstarch paste to the stew. Stir and allow to boil again, stirring constantly, until thickened. Cook for a final 3 minutes before serving.

KIDNEY BEANS

Sautéed Flageolet Beans with Fusilli.

Tagliatelle with Lentil Sauce

Here's a handy recipe you can rustle up in minutes.

OPPOSITE *Tagliatelle with Lentil Sauce.*

SERVES 4

¾lb dried tagliatelle

dash of olive oil

2 tbsp butter

FOR THE SAUCE:

2 tbsp olive oil

2 cloves of garlic, crushed

1 large onion, very finely chopped

1 generous cup red lentils, washed and drained

3 tbsp tomato paste

salt and freshly ground black pepper

2½ cups boiling water

sprigs of fresh rosemary, to garnish

freshly grated Parmesan cheese, to serve

Bring a large saucepan of water to the boil, and add the tagliatelle with a dash of olive oil. Cook for about 10 minutes, stirring occasionally, until tender. Drain, and return to the saucepan. Add the butter and stir. Cover and set aside, to keep warm.

To make the lentil sauce, heat the olive oil in a large saucepan and sauté the garlic and onion for about 5 minutes, stirring occasionally, until softened. Add the lentils, tomato paste, salt and freshly ground black pepper, and stir in the boiling water. Bring to the boil, then simmer for about 20 minutes, stirring occasionally, until the lentils have softened.

Reheat the tagliatelle gently for 2–3 minutes, if necessary, then serve with the lentil sauce. Scatter a few sprigs of fresh rosemary over the top, and serve with freshly grated Parmesan cheese.

Store-cupboard Salad

Use tiny pasta shapes for this salad and serve with warm, crusty French bread.

FLAGEOLET BEANS

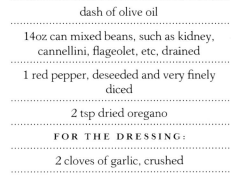

SERVES 4–6

½ cup dried pastina (tiny shapes)

dash of olive oil

14oz can mixed beans, such as kidney, cannellini, flageolet, etc, drained

1 red pepper, deseeded and very finely diced

2 tsp dried oregano

FOR THE DRESSING:

2 cloves of garlic, crushed

4 tbsp extra virgin olive oil

2–3 tbsp balsamic vinegar

1 tsp tomato paste

salt and freshly ground black pepper

Bring a large saucepan of water to the boil, and add the pastina with a dash of olive oil. Cook for about 8 minutes, stirring occasionally, until tender. Drain, and rinse under cold running water. Drain again, and place in a large mixing bowl.

Add the beans, red pepper, and oregano to the pasta. Place all the dressing ingredients in a screw-top jar, and shake well to combine. Pour the dressing over the salad, toss, and chill for at least 30 minutes before serving.

Continental Lentil Soup

Canned lentils make this soup even easier to prepare. They are available from most good delicatessens.

FUSILLI

SERVES 4–6

¼ cup butter

2 cloves of garlic, crushed

⅓ cup dried pastina (any tiny shapes)

4 tbsp finely chopped, fresh parsley

14oz can brown lentils, drained

6½ cups vegetable broth

salt and freshly ground black pepper

freshly grated Parmesan cheese, to serve (optional)

Melt the butter in a large saucepan and sauté the garlic for about 2 minutes, stirring occasionally.

Add the pastina and chopped parsley, and stir. Cook for a further 2–3 minutes, then add the lentils and stock, and season with salt and freshly ground black pepper.

Bring the soup to the boil, then reduce the heat and simmer for about 15 minutes. Serve with a little freshly grated Parmesan cheese, if wished.

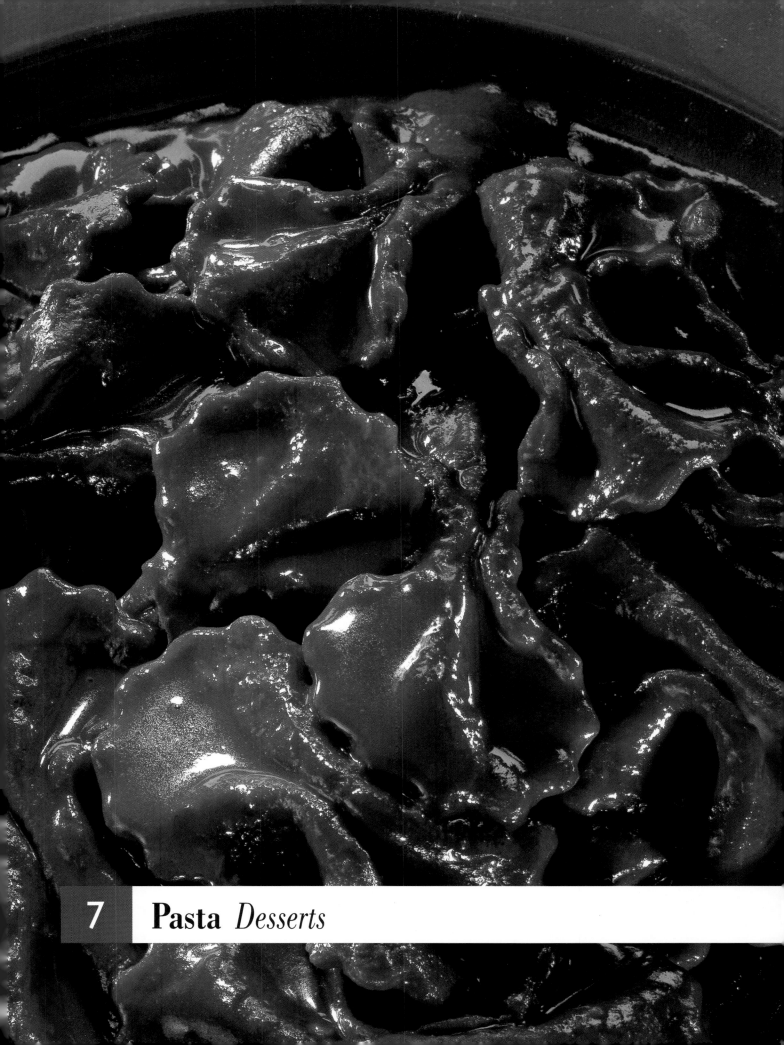

7   **Pasta** *Desserts*

Baked Pasta Pudding

This unsophisticated dessert will probably become a firm favorite with the adults as well as children.

FIGS

SERVES 4

¼lb dried tagliatelle

dash of sunflower oil

¼ cup butter

2 eggs

½ cup sugar

pinch of cinnamon

grated zest of 1 lemon

few drops of vanilla essence

4 tbsp seedless raisins

sifted powdered sugar, to decorate

Preheat the oven to 375°F. Bring a large saucepan of water to the boil, and add the tagliatelle with a dash of sunflower oil. Cook for about 10 minutes, stirring occasionally, until tender. Drain, and rinse under cold running water. Drain again, and set aside.

Place the butter in a shallow, ovenproof dish, and melt in the oven for about 5 minutes. Remove from the oven, and carefully swirl the melted butter around the sides of the dish. Set aside to cool slightly.

In a mixing bowl, whisk together the eggs and sugar until thick and frothy. Whisk in the cinnamon, lemon zest, vanilla essence, and reserved melted butter. Stir in the seedless raisins and cooked tagliatelle until evenly coated in the egg mixture.

Transfer the pudding mixture to the prepared dish, and distribute evenly. Bake for about 35–40 minutes, until the mixture has set and is crisp and golden. Allow to cool slightly. Serve warm, decorated with sifted powdered sugar.

Honey, Orange, and Almond Tagliatelle

Here's a really quick and easy dessert. Pasta tossed in butter and honey syrup makes a perfect pasta dish to end a meal.

SERVES 4–6

½lb dried egg tagliatelle

dash of sunflower oil

4 oranges

5 tbsp clear honey

3 tbsp soft light brown sugar

1 tbsp lemon juice

3 tbsp butter

⅔ cup flaked almonds

Bring a large saucepan of water to the boil, and add the tagliatelle with a dash of sunflower oil. Cook for about 8–10 minutes, stirring occasionally, until tender. Drain, and set aside.

While the pasta is cooking, peel and slice three of the oranges, and cut the slices in half. Squeeze the juice from the remaining orange into a small saucepan. Add the honey, sugar, and lemon juice. Bring to the boil, stirring to dissolve the sugar, and simmer for 1–2 minutes, until syrupy.

Melt the butter in a large frying pan, and fry the flaked almonds until golden. Stir in the tagliatelle and honey syrup, heat through, then quickly stir in the orange slices. Serve immediately.

TIP:

Pare strips of zest from the skin of one orange, and cut into thin "julienne" strips for decoration.

Chocolate Pasta Torte

A decadently rich dessert to serve on special occasions. Use good-quality plain dessert chocolate – ordinary cooking chocolate just won't taste the same.

SERVES 8

generous ¼lb dried vermicelli (thin spaghetti)

dash of sunflower oil, plus extra for greasing

12oz plain chocolate, broken into pieces

4 tbsp water

½ cup unsalted butter

½ cup sugar

finely grated zest of 1 orange

8oz can unsweetened chestnut purée

4 tbsp brandy

⅔ cup ground almonds

½ cup flaked almonds

5 tbsp heavy cream

chocolate leaves, to decorate

Bring a large saucepan of water to the boil, and add the vermicelli with a dash of sunflower oil. Cook for about 6 minutes, stirring occasionally, until tender. Drain, and rinse under cold running water. Drain again, and set aside.

Lightly oil a 7-inch round springform or loose-bottomed cake tin and line with waxed paper. Lightly oil the paper.

Place 8oz chocolate and the water in a small saucepan, and heat gently until melted. Set aside to cool.

Meanwhile, cream together the butter, sugar, and orange zest until light and fluffy, then gradually beat in the chestnut purée.

Add the melted chocolate to the brandy, and mix well. Stir in the almonds and cooked vermicelli. Turn the mixture into the prepared tin and smooth over the surface. Refrigerate overnight.

Put the remaining chocolate and the cream into a small bowl over a saucepan of simmering water and heat gently, stirring occasionally, until melted and smooth. Remove the bowl from the heat.

Remove the torte from the tin, and place on a wire cooling rack. Pour the melted chocolate mixture evenly over the cake, using a palette knife to coat the sides. Leave to set.

Carefully transfer the torte to a serving plate, and decorate with chocolate leaves.

TIP:
To make chocolate leaves, melt 2oz white or milk dessert chocolate in a small bowl over a saucepan of simmering water. Using a small brush, paint the melted chocolate onto the backs of a selection of small leaves. Arrange on a baking sheet lined with waxed paper, and leave to set for at least 2 hours at room temperature. Carefully peel away the leaves and discard.

PEARS

Fruit Ravioli with a Red Coulis

Look out for dried mango and pineapple in health food shops and delicatessens. Alternatively, use a mixture of chopped candied fruits in this recipe.

SERVES 6–8

FOR THE FILLING:

about 15 ready-to-eat dried apricots, finely chopped

⅔ cup dried mango or pineapple, finely chopped

finely grated zest of 1 orange

½ tsp cinnamon

2 tbsp amaretto liqueur (optional)

⅔ quantity Pasta Dough (page 8), omitting the salt, using 1 tbsp fresh orange juice instead of the water, and adding the finely grated zest of 1 orange to the eggs

lightly beaten egg

dash of sunflower oil

FOR THE COULIS:

¾lb fresh raspberries

½ cup powdered sugar, sifted

TO DECORATE:

finely chopped pistachio nuts

fresh raspberries

mint sprigs

First make the filling; mix together the apricots, dried mango or pineapple, orange zest, and cinnamon and set aside. Add the amaretto, if desired.

To make the ravioli, cut the pasta dough in half, and roll out one half to a 14 × 10-inch rectangle. Trim the edges of the dough, and cover with plastic wrap to prevent it from drying out.

Roll out the other piece of pasta dough to the same size. Place half teaspoonfuls of the filling mixture in lines ¾-inch apart on one piece of dough. Lightly brush beaten egg between the filling mixture, and carefully lay the second piece of dough over the top. Starting at one end, press the dough down around the filling, carefully pushing out any trapped air. Using a sharp knife, pastry wheel or round cutter, cut in lines between the filling to divide the ravioli into squares.

Cook the ravioli in a large saucepan of boiling water with a dash of sunflower oil for about 5 minutes, stirring occasionally, until tender. Drain, and set aside to cool slightly.

Meanwhile, make the coulis; place the raspberries and powdered sugar in a food processor or blender, and purée until smooth. Sieve to remove the seeds.

Serve the ravioli on individual plates with the coulis, and decorate with chopped pistachio nuts, fresh raspberries, and mint sprigs.

RASPBERRIES

Chocolate Pasta with Chocolate Sauce

A chocoholic's dream – it has to be tasted to be believed!

⅔ quantity Pasta Dough (page 8), omitting the salt and adding ¼ cup cocoa powder and 3 tbsp powdered sugar to the flour

dash of sunflower oil

FOR THE SAUCE:

6oz bar plain chocolate, broken into pieces

⅔ cup milk

2 tbsp corn syrup

2 tbsp butter

TO DECORATE:

fresh strawberries

amaretti biscuits

FIGS

Keep the pasta dough wrapped in plastic wrap to prevent it drying out, and set aside.

To make the sauce, place all the ingredients in a small saucepan and heat gently, stirring, for about 5 minutes, until melted, smooth, and shiny. Cool slightly.

Roll out the pasta dough thinly on a floured surface, and cut into rounds with a 2-inch round plain or fluted cutter. Pinch the sides of each dough round together, pleating in the middle to make a bow shape. Set the bows aside on baking sheets lined with waxed paper.

To cook the pasta bows, bring a large saucepan of water to the boil, and add the pasta with a dash of sunflower oil. Cook for about 3 minutes, stirring occasionally, until tender. Drain, and return to the saucepan.

Pour the chocolate sauce over the pasta, and stir gently to coat.

Winter Fruit Compote with Tiny Pasta Shapes

Try this for breakfast. It needs to be started the day before, and will keep for several days in the refrigerator. Make up your own selection of mixed dried fruit, if you prefer.

SERVES 4–6

about 15 dried apricots

1¼ cups dried apple rings or chunks

about 12 dried pears

8 dried figs

50g/2oz dried cherries

4 cloves

2 allspice berries

1 cinnamon stick

finely grated zest and juice of 1 orange

1¼ cups weak tea

⅔ cup water

3 tbsp soft brown sugar

4 tbsp dried pastina (any tiny shapes)

Place the dried fruit in a bowl with the spices, orange zest and juice, tea and water. Cover, and leave to soak overnight.

The next day, spoon the compote into a saucepan, bring to the boil, and simmer for 15 minutes, adding a little more water if necessary. Stir in the brown sugar and pastina, and cook for a further 8–10 minutes, until the pastina is tender. Serve warm or cold.

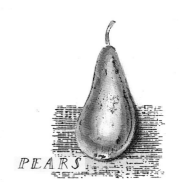

PEARS

Cinnamon Fettuccine
with Apple and Cinnamon Sauce

This delightful autumn dessert is delicious served with cream. Ground mixed spice makes a good alternative to cinnamon.

SERVES 6

⅔ quantity Pasta Dough (page 8), (omitting the salt and adding 2 tsp ground cinnamon to the flour)

FOR THE SAUCE:

3–4 medium dessert apples, peeled, cored, and sliced

finely grated zest of 1 lemon

¼ tsp ground cinnamon

3 tbsp water, plus ⅔ cup

3 tbsp soft light brown sugar

½ cup seedless raisins

1 tbsp butter, plus a little extra

2 tsp arrowroot blended with 2 tsp cold water

flour, to dredge

dash of sunflower oil

Keep the pasta dough wrapped in plastic wrap to prevent it from drying out, and set aside.

To make the sauce, put the apples into a saucepan with the lemon zest, cinnamon, and 3 tbsp water. Cover, and cook gently until the apples have softened. Remove about half of the apple slices from the saucepan, and set aside. Place the remaining apples in a food processor or blender, and purée until smooth.

Return the purée to the saucepan and stir in the reserved apples, sugar, seedless raisins, 1 tbsp butter, arrowroot mixture, and ⅔ cup water. Cook for about 5 minutes, stirring constantly, until bubbling and thickened. Set aside.

To make the fettuccine, roll out the pasta dough very thinly on a floured surface. Lightly dredge with flour, then roll up and use a sharp knife to cut the dough into ¼-inch wide slices. Shake out the noodles as they are cut, and pile them on a floured baking tray.

To cook the fettuccine, bring a large saucepan of water to the boil and add the pasta with a dash of sunflower oil. Cook for about 3 minutes, stirring occasionally, until tender.

Meanwhile, reheat the sauce. Drain the fettuccine, and toss with a little extra butter. Stir in the sauce, and serve on warmed individual plates.

> **TIP:**
> For a special occasion, sprinkle each plate of pasta with a little calvados or rum before serving.

RASPBERRIES

Index

TARRAGON